"Just imagine you're not a Beatles fan, but you find yourself grieving over the untimely death of John Lennon.

Just imagine your grief is so overwhelming your life falls apart. Are you crazy or is there a deeper, stranger reason?

This was the dilemma of Jewelle St. James, a Canadian housewife and mother.

And just imagine her surprise and awe when, in her search for answers, she finds the explanation in historical England.

Her journey in this life is rooted in a past life. And the emotional yet satisfying answer that love never dies is for all our journeys into the next life."

——SHARON JARVIS, Literary Agent

"In *All You Need Is Love*, Jewelle St. James shares with us her remarkable journey into the worlds of spirituality and reincarnation. Using meticulous real-world research to test the validity of her own hunches, intuition, and highly personal messages from beyond, Jewelle firmly establishes that her bond to John Lennon in this lifetime is rooted in lives they led centuries ago, and that the real love they shared way back when, continues to this day."

——SUZANE NORTHROP, Author of
Everything Happens for a Reason

ALL YOU NEED IS LOVE – SECOND EDITION

is Available on Amazon and Amazon Kindle.

John Lennon *and the* Brontë Connection

Is ex-Beatle John Lennon the reincarnation of the troubled Branwell Brontë, brother to England's most literary sisters?

Jewelle St. James

Library and Archives Canada Cataloguing in Publication
St. James, Jewelle, 1953–
[Lennon-Brontë connection]
    John Lennon and the Brontë connection / Jewelle St. James.

Previosuly published under title: The Lennon-Brontë connection.
"Is ex-Beatle John Lennon the reincarnation of the troubled
    Branwell Brontë, brother to England's most literary sisters?"
Includes bibliographical references.
Issued in print and electronic formats.
ISBN 978-0-9732752-6-1 (paperback)
ISBN 978-0-9732752-7-8 (html)

    1. Reincarnation. 2. Reincarnation—Biography. 3. Spiritual life.
4. Brontë, Patrick Branwell, 1817–1848. 5. Lennon, John, 1940–1980.
6. St. James, Jewelle, 1953–. I. Title. II. Title: Lennon-Brontë connection.
BL515.S75 2015   133.901'35   C2015-902540-0
                                                 C2015-902541-9

Front cover image: Self portrait of Patrick Branwell Brontë –
    'Courtesy of The Brontë Society'
Editing by Ann Harmer
Book design by Fiona Raven
Author's cover photo: All rights reserved

First Printing, May 2015
Printed in Canada

St. James Publishing
bcauthor@icloud.com

For Dayle Sheridan
with love

Acknowledgements

Thank you:

To the spirit of John Baron—with love always.

To Gerry, my dearest soul sister.

To my wise and wonderful mentors: France Allion, Mary Noll, and Dayle Sheridan.

Thank you dear France for this book's Afterword.

To fellow writers who, through the years, have made my world a richer place:
Shelley Germeaux, Judy Hall, Bill Harry, Peter Jerrome, Linda Keen, Jason Leen, Barry McGuinness, Dennis McMahon, Stephen Sakellarios, Dee Silverstein, Jan Tober, Eve A. Thomas, Patricia Walker, and Sherry Ann White.

To dedicated Brontë biographers and experts, both past and present, for providing literary subsistence for which this author is most grateful:

Dr. Juliet Barker, Ann Dinsdale, Daphne Du Maurier, Francis H. Grundy, Alice Law, Francis A. Leyland, Imelda Marsden, A. Mary F. Robinson.

In memory of my parents, Lillyean O. Walle and Henry John Walle, and my dear sister Konni Frazier.

To Jack and Renee Brodie who remain dear to my heart.

To friends who have each played a unique role in my journey: Herma Daley, Len and Ann Bargus, Ros Staker, Myra Wendy, and Ann Boxall.

Also, Monika Evans, Karin Jander, Christine Patterson, and Glenna Quinn.

To Ann Harmer for excellent editing, and a special thank you for writing this book's Foreword.

To Fiona Raven for a beautiful book design, typesetting, and more. You're truly the best !

Thank you for generous assistance and kind permissions from:

The Brontë Parsonage Museum, and the Brontë Society:
http://www.bronte.org.uk/

The British Newspaper Archive:
http://www.britishnewspaperarchive.co.uk/

Barry McGuinness: http://personalityspirituality.net/

Huddersfield Daily Examiner, Yorkshire:
http://www.examiner.co.uk/

Getty Images: http://www.gettyimages.com

Ann Dinsdale, Author of *The Brontës at Haworth*

St. Martin's Press, New York City

JUJAMCYN Theaters, New York City

Black Bull Pub, Haworth, Yorkshire, England

John Baron has proved that Love lasts Forever

——Myra Wendy, West Sussex, England

Excerpt from

EMILY BRONTË *(1883)*

by A. Mary F. Robinson

ALREADY BY THE 29th of October of this melancholy year of 1848 Emily's cough and cold had made such progress as to alarm her careful older sister. Before Branwell's death she had been, to all appearance, the one strong member of a delicate family. By the side of fragile Anne (already, did they but know it, advanced in tubercular consumption), of shattered Branwell, of Charlotte, ever nervous and ailing, this tall, muscular Emily had appeared a tower of strength. Working early and late, seldom tired and never complaining, finding her best relaxation in long, rough walks on the moors, she seemed unlikely to give them any poignant anxiety. But the seeds of phthisis lay deep down beneath this far show of life and strength; the shock of sorrow which she experienced for her brother's death developed them with alarming rapidity.

The weariness of absence had always proved too much for Emily's strength. Away from home we have seen how she pined and sickened. Exile made her thin and wan, menaced the very springs of life. And now she must endure an inevitable and unending absence, an exile from which there could be no return. The strain was too tight, the wrench too sharp: Emily could not bear it and live. To such a loss of hers, bereaved of a helpless sufferer, the mourning of those who remain is embittered and quickened a hundred times a day when the blank minutes come round for which the customary duties are missing, when the unwelcome leisure hangs round the weary soul like a shapeless and encumbering garment. It was Emily who had chiefly devoted herself to Branwell. He being dead, the motive of her life seemed gone.

Foreword

by Ann Harmer

WHEN JEWELLE ST. JAMES began receiving messages from John Lennon after his death, she knew very little about the life of this man; she had remained untouched by his music and unswayed by his influence. But the messages continued, insistent and frequent, until she could no longer ignore them.

So Jewelle followed his beckoning, albeit unwillingly at first, and discovered that she and John had not only shared past lives in seventeenth-century England, they had also shared a deep and abiding love. Jewelle chronicled this experience in her book *All You Need Is Love*.

After the book was published, it was time for Jewelle to get on with her life in a quiet mountain town in western Canada. But life had other plans. Finally, still unsure but willing to pay heed to John's continuing "spirit messages," she took up a new life in a new town among people who believed in and respected these psychic communications.

And so began the next stage of Jewelle's uncommon present-life/past-life story.

She was now receiving messages pointing to a connection with the Brontës, the well-known literary family of the Yorkshire moors. Jewelle came to learn that she and John Lennon shared another past lifetime, she as Emily Brontë (the author of *Wuthering Heights*) and he as Branwell Brontë, the brilliant but troubled brother of the better-known sisters.

We continue to follow the author on her own personal journey, from confusion and unwillingness to ultimate acceptance of her role in an unfolding story, a story in which John Lennon and Jewelle St. James share a connection that reaches beyond today's physical world.

One

"*The Catcher in the Rye,*" she murmured.

My eldest daughter, Joanne, had called—this was in October of 2011—and asked, "Would you like to visit New York City?" She explained that her daughter's school group needed chaperones for their upcoming spring-break trip to New York.

I had always wanted to see the city that John Lennon had loved and where he had died, yet for many reasons the journey seemed too daunting to tackle.

In the middle of our phone conversation, Joanne said absentmindedly, "*The Catcher in the Rye.*"

"Why did you say that?" I sputtered.

"Oh," said my multi-tasking daughter, "I'm reading the

cover of the school's book-club magazine. You know, the ones sent home with kids, encouraging them to read?"

"Do you *know* about that book?" I asked.

Joanne began to explain the gist of *The Catcher in the Rye*.

"No, no," I interrupted. "The killer was carrying *The Catcher in the Rye* when he shot John Lennon."

"Oh," Joanne said quietly. "I didn't know that."

The mention of *The Catcher in the Rye* felt like a password, leaving me no choice but to accept the invitation to visit John's beloved New York City.

In 2009, when an unexpected out-of-town job offer came my way, it was my chance to start a new life away from the mountain town that had been home. The Vancouver suburb, where I would be living with and taking care of an elderly English couple, was chock-full of British residents. I dubbed the beautiful area "Little England."

Despite years of discovering past-life evidence and experiencing spirit communication, my mind still doubted sometimes. Yet the new couple, Jack and Renee, understood the metaphysical world.

Renee was a spiritual teacher and author, and Jack was a highly intelligent skeptic who would challenge all theories and opinions, then surprise you with his deeply insightful conclusions about life.

For seven months I was Renee's caregiver, learning much from this lovely woman, a true "English rose."

Renee, who looked to the Light bringing love and positive vibrations to life's situations, said we all had a job to do, our life's purpose, and that we shouldn't worry about being judged by others. Asked if she ever worried about criticism of her spiritual work, she replied, "No, I was just doing what I was meant to do. Period. You're bound to have some criticism, but it shouldn't matter to you, only to the person criticizing."

When Renee passed away, I felt fortunate to have learned so much from her. Little did I know that her husband, Jack, who was the age of my own departed father, and who now needed a caregiver himself, would play an unforgettable role in my life.

Jack was a "proper English gentleman" who retained much of his Victorian upbringing in his values and lifestyle. His main interests in life, other than love for his family, were politics and the environment.

Therefore, after I arrived in Little England, lingering doubts about my spirit guide's presence melted away, resulting in a (mostly) crystal-clear channel. I felt as if the previous twenty-five years of my life had been a partially obstructed river contaminated with doubt, allowing only a trickle of spiritual information through. Then in 2009 the floodgates opened, and to this day, never-ending spirit communication flows through me.

I wasn't sure about what was ahead, though. I had shared my past life through my books, and I now pondered my long-term future. I was now accustomed to the "little voice" that felt like a sixth sense, the same voice that had been guiding my life for years.

One day, while window shopping, I again wondered about the future. What should I do now that the books had been written? A new occupation, perhaps? The voice suggested going to a nearby thrift shop. I knew these directions were from my guide and long-lost love, Mr. John Baron.

I entered the thrift shop and, a new occupation still on my mind, immediately spotted a table displaying some upright books. The tallest was titled, *Do What You Are— Discover the Perfect Career for You through the Secrets of Personality Type.* A smaller pocketbook in front of that one was titled, *Jewel.*

This was typical of the way Spirit-John presented his signs and messages. I smiled, then mulled over my earlier question, *What should I do with my life?*

Answer: *Jewel, do what you are.*

But what did that mean, "Do what you are?" What was I? I examined the personality-type book more closely and gulped. One of the authors' names was Barbara Barron.

These days, I differentiate less between John Lennon and John Baron—they are both simply "John."

When John said (telepathically), *become re-acquainted*

with the Brontës, I obliged. Or so I thought at the time. Spirit-John said other things too, how Jack was John's father from another lifetime. I wondered if John meant William Baron, John Baron's father from Wiltshire in the 1600s.

It didn't occur to me that John meant *another* past-life father.

Two

BEFORE LEAVING THE mountain town, I had a sense that John had certain information to share. After I moved to Little England and "connected" with him, he asked, *"Are you ready for the big L?"*

"The big *L?*" I laughed. "Lennon?"

In my head he seemed to reply, *"Love. Leap. A leap of faith."*

Was I ready for a leap of faith? Probably not.

Time passed as I waited for the other shoe to drop, until I pleaded into thin air, "Well, which direction *do* I take?"

A thought came in a flash: *Get re-acquainted with the Brontës.*

The Brontës? I hadn't thought about them for a long

time. *Well okay, I'll get re-acquainted with the Brontës.* But I didn't take the idea too seriously.

I made a cup of tea and checked my email. A message had arrived from a stranger, Barry McGuinness, a psychologist from Bath, England. Barry introduced himself and his fascinating website that compared celebrities' current and past lives. He was excited to have discovered in *All You Need Is Love* that John Lennon and Branwell Brontë were possibly the same soul. Barry had expanded on my theory by posting photos of Lennon and Brontë, featuring their uncanny physical resemblances.

An excellent psychic (Glenna Quinn) once suggested that my spirit-guide usually has to "shout" to get through. I quickly forgot about Barry's email and perhaps chose subconsciously to ignore Spirit-John's earlier suggestion that I become re-acquainted with the Brontës. Yet one day I again pleaded, "What direction am I to take?"

That afternoon I received an email from a friend, Moira.

I *never* hear from Moira, so it was a shock to see her email and the subject line: Branwell Brontë. Moira had a book about him and wondered if I was still interested in him.

My cousin called on the same April afternoon. She had a package to deliver. Could I meet her that same night? I was puzzled—we had visited just days before, and public transit takes forever from her place to mine, but she insisted on bringing the package.

I felt unsettled. Moira's uncanny timing of the Branwell email was still on my mind. I turned the TV on to *The Oprah Winfrey Show*. She was interviewing a young woman about the hazards of sending text messages while driving. The interviewee's first name appeared on the screen: *Bronte*.

Over our pot of tea, I shared the day's events: asking John for direction, Moira's Branwell email, and Oprah's guest, Bronte. My relative's face had an odd expression as she handed me the "urgent" package. I ripped it open and tears sprang to my eyes. The package contained a box of English biscuits, and on the box was a depiction of Haworth village, the Brontës' home.

Weeks later I asked why she had delivered the box of "Haworth English biscuits" on that particular day. "I have no answer," she laughed, "except there seemed an urgency to bring it *that* day." This was an example of how, through the years, an avalanche of multiple messages will appear, and as Glenna described, "Your spirit guide often has to 'shout' to get your attention."

Over several years, Barry McGuinness and I have discussed Emily Brontë, yet at my request he never mentioned this on his website. However, when I finally gave him the thumbs-up and he posted an article with comparison photos, I nearly died of embarrassment. But I trusted him, and if anyone was going to explain a case study about Emily Brontë, he was the right choice for me.

SOUL MATES:
THE REINCARNATION OF EMILY BRONTË
by Barry McGuinness

Excerpts: The full article and comparison photos can be seen at
http://personalityspirituality.net/2011/12/18/soul-mates-the-
reincarnation-of-emily-bronte/

Although she herself is very reluctant to admit it, everything points to an ordinary Canadian woman having been this famous novelist in a previous life. Whenever someone claims to be the reincarnation of a well-known historical personality, a healthy dose of scepticism is generally required. I have lost count of the number of people claiming to be the reincarnation of Jesus, for instance.

This case is absolutely not one of these.

There is a strong likelihood that Jewelle St. James, a health-care worker from British Columbia, is the reincarnation of the nineteenth-century novelist Emily Brontë, author of *Wuthering Heights*.

Yet Jewelle herself, despite having written several books on her search to uncover past lives, has been most reluctant of all to accept this, and even since coming to terms with it she has been highly resistant to disclosing anything about it. To this day, she has not made any public reference to it.

She has, however, given me permission to tell the story.

An Inexplicable Grief

Readers familiar with Jewelle's books will know that her own awakening to past lives began on December 8, 1980, with the murder of John Lennon.

On hearing of his death, something deep inside her was stirred up—even though she had never known or met Lennon, and had never really been a major Beatles fan. She felt—inexplicably—as though she had lost someone very dear and very close.

And that feeling refused to go away. In fact, she was beside herself with grief for the next three years, something which many friends and family found incomprehensible.

Jewelle has spent much of the last three decades getting to the bottom of this mystery. And through a mixture of psychic readings, personal experiences and dogged research, she has uncovered a number of fascinating lives—including at least two that her soul happens to have shared with the soul that eventually became known as John Lennon.

This discovery practically forced itself upon Jewelle, despite the fact that she was, to begin with, unsure about reincarnation *and* highly embarrassed by the suggestion of having had a past life connected with someone famous. But her continued investigations led not only to one validation after another but also to personal insights and emotional healing.

John Baron and Katherine James

For years, different psychics have consistently given Jewelle information concerning two past lives involving John Lennon.

First, she learned that the soul of John Lennon had once lived in seventeenth-century England as a man by the name of John Baron—and that Jewelle had been John Baron's beloved girlfriend. She was a Sussex girl known as Katherine who worked in a local infirmary tending the sick and dying.

Amazingly, through her investigations in England, Jewelle was able to verify the actual recorded identity of this individual: she was a Ms. Katherine James from the small market town of Petworth in the county of Sussex. She was born in 1666 and died in her teens in 1683.

Jewelle learned that Katherine had died while in love with John Baron. The relationship had ended in tragedy, and resonances from that life appeared to have haunted much of Jewelle's present life —right up to the inexplicable grief over John Lennon's death.

Branwell and Emily Brontë

Another thing Jewelle was repeatedly told by various psychics was that, two centuries later, John Lennon had been the lesser known brother of the famous Brontë sisters, a tragic fellow by the name of Branwell Brontë (1817–1848).

Following up on this lead, it was Jewelle herself who first discovered the many remarkable similarities between Branwell Brontë and John Lennon. She then wrote about these developments in her book *All You Need Is Love*.

But in that book, I noticed, the various psychics had given clues about her own identity at the time of Branwell.

At least one appeared to suggest that she herself had been one of Branwell's sisters. And another gave the letters *E.B.* as the initials of her name.

Putting two and two together, it was implied that

Jewelle had been Emily Brontë. Yet Jewelle did not discuss the possibility at all in her book.

I contacted Jewelle in August 2009 to enquire about this. She confirmed that the same psychics who were picking up on the connection between John Lennon and Branwell Brontë were also telling her explicitly about her own past life as Emily Brontë.

> "Usually a reading will go like this: I ask about John and Branwell and they immediately forget about Branwell and say, 'And you were Emily.'"

But Jewelle also explained that she had deliberately avoided opening this particular can of worms in her writing:

> "For years, decades actually, while I investigated the past life with John Lennon, I was afraid to boldly announce my connection to him, so to state a Brontë life as well, it seemed to be pushing the envelope . . ."

Perhaps it should come as no surprise, but this very reticence is something she shares with Emily Brontë.

The reclusive writer

Emily Brontë (1818–1848) was the middle one of three sisters (Charlotte, Emily and Anne) who survived into adulthood, two others having died in childhood.

The Brontë girls and their brother lived with their parents in the Yorkshire village of Haworth, a place surrounded by desolate moorland.

Always very shy, very private, and very reclusive, Emily had no friends to speak of and rarely ventured away from home except to stride around the moors with her dog. This is where she felt most at peace. It is said that she had almost a spiritual relationship to the moors, a sentiment that comes across in her outstanding novel *Wuthering Heights*.

During my correspondence with Jewelle, I put together for her some comparisons of the faces of John Lennon and Branwell Brontë. I then also did comparisons using photos of Jewelle in her twenties and portraits of Emily Brontë at similar ages.

I feel there is a strong resemblance between Emily Brontë and Jewelle St. James, just as there is between the faces of Branwell Brontë and John Lennon.

Wuthering Heights

Looking at Emily's great novel in the context of reincarnation, *Wuthering Heights* shows a few interesting resonances with the lives of John Baron and Katherine James two centuries earlier. The story revolves around the intense but ultimately doomed love between a Yorkshire farm girl, Cathy, and her adopted brother, possibly of Gypsy origin, the notorious Heathcliff.

Far from the nice, Jane Austen-style romance, this is a staggeringly dark and brutal tale of love, hate, abuse, revenge and death.

At first, the novel was dismissed outright by critics. It just seemed far too intense and amoral for the gentlefolk of Victorian England. Neglected and misunderstood, Emily died without hearing any acclaim for her work.

As with the lives of John Baron and Katherine James in seventeenth-century Sussex, in *Wuthering Heights* we have soul mates who feel they belong together but are tragically unable to do so. It is interesting to note that Emily named her heroine Catherine, and that a psychic once described John Baron to Jewelle as a bit of a Heathcliff character. Perhaps that earlier life of doomed love was, subconsciously, an inspiration for Emily's writing.

Another likely inspiration for the Heathcliff character is the reincarnation of John Baron, Emily's own brother Branwell—a gifted but tortured soul who had failed to live up to the expectations of his talented family. Although the unfortunate Branwell eventually ruined himself with excessive drinking, Emily (the reincarnation of Katherine James) never stopped caring for him. It is said that she waited up for him every night and carried him up to his room when he was too drunk to get there himself.

If John Baron and Branwell Brontë were indeed one and the same soul, then it would be strangely fitting on various levels if Branwell inspired some of the Heathcliff character conceived by Emily.

And then of course we have John Lennon—a rock star who was not only famously outspoken but also managed to turn his personal anger into public art, a rallying cry for the masses to change the world. My guess is that the Baron/Brontë/Lennon soul was carrying some kind of anger against society which, as John Lennon, finally became channeled into something creative rather than self-destructive.

Interestingly, Emily Brontë died very shortly after Branwell Brontë just as Katherine James had died very shortly after John Baron—a pattern that did not repeat this time with the death of John Lennon.

Jewelle and John Lennon never met—their lives had no intersection this time around. Presumably that was planned for some reason—after all, we do not spend every lifetime relating to the same soul mates. But perhaps they will incarnate together again in some future lifetime...

Three

IN THE SPRING of 2012 I joined my granddaughter and her school group for a whirlwind tour of New York City. We loved New York. What a wonderful city! The sights and energy were more than we ever imagined, yet I braced myself before visiting the entrance to the Dakota apartment building where John Lennon had been murdered that December night in 1980.

I'd read somewhere that congestion from tour buses outside the Dakota were a problem for local residents. I longed to see where John's life had ended, yet I hoped *not* to see the place through a bus window.

One night after attending a Broadway play, we stood near Times Square, absorbing the hundreds of flashing lights, neon billboards, crowds, and noise. We'd just seen *Memphis,* and I wondered how many people in the audience had shed tears over the play's message of sharing one's own unique and individual gifts in life, that your inner self knows and carries that knowledge even when it seems the world has other ideas.

A theater sign in the distance, amidst a hundred flashing neon signs, caught my eye: *St. James Leap of Faith*

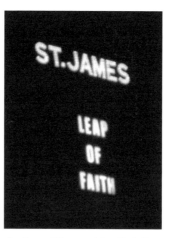

St. James Theatre, New York City

Was I seeing things?

My young companion confirmed the illuminated words: *St. James—Leap of Faith.* She snapped a photo and kept repeating, "Grandma, it's a message for you. I can't believe it!" Directly below the Leap of Faith sign was a smaller (blurry to me) neon sign that seemed to read:

John's Pizzeria

As if reading my mind, my granddaughter squealed, "It says John!"

The next day brought us to the Dakota Apartments. Our tour guide dropped us near a café on West 72nd Street. After a quick bite, we would walk to the Dakota and Central Park. It was a warm spring day—magnolia trees and flowers were in blossom—and I was relieved to approach John's former home by foot and *not* observe this sacred place from the window of a tour bus.

We lagged far behind our tour group because my granddaughter had spotted a newspaper stand and wanted a souvenir copy of the *New York Times* for her father. She was taking too much time, and I was antsy to get going. I joined her at the newspaper stand, hoping to speed things along.

A sign plastered on the newsstand said *Barron's* and later, as we hastened down the street, I felt that was a reminder: Lennon *is* Baron, so relax, everything will be fine.

My only distraction at the gothic-looking Dakota Apartments was a US one-dollar bill lying on the sidewalk across from where John had been shot. I stuffed the bill into my pocket.

We craned our necks toward a balcony in the sky. Our tour guide said that John Lennon's widow, Yoko Ono, lived in that apartment.

I could feel John. His spirit soared high above Central Park. He was happy and at peace. Or so it felt to me.

Then a light-bulb moment: John Lennon was *one* lifetime of John's soul. John Lennon was (obviously) John Lennon until he died, and then he returned to all that he *is*—to all that he has *ever been*, like we too will one day reunite with the larger part of ourselves. In that second, I understood the years of sadness, of feeling foolish and embarrassed over my deep conviction that John in spirit was communicating and guiding my life. Because John's spirit now encompasses his many lifetimes of "expressions," he can communicate with me (and others) through his various past-life personalities.

In that split second outside the Dakota Apartments, my understanding was crystal clear. I've always struggled, getting my head around Baron (and Brontë) being Lennon, so when he communicated, I could only accept John Baron.

Now, after thirty years, I finally understood! When John communicates, it's not necessarily Beatle-John speaking. He's all who John has ever been, and that *does* include Beatle-John. I had to travel all the way to New York City to truly "get it."

As in *A Christmas Carol* (1843), by Charles Dickens, when Ebenezer Scrooge awakens after contact with the spirits of Christmas past, present, and future, jolting him to his senses, I too came to my senses and *finally* no longer feel embarrassed about having had a past life with the soul who became John Lennon.

The scent of waving bluebells filled the air as we entered Central Park and strolled through Strawberry Fields, an area dedicated to the memory of John Lennon, a most beautiful place where peace reigns.

Days later and hours before flying home, we sat at a café in the Metropolitan Museum of Art, overlooking Central Park. I asked my intuitive granddaughter about finding the one-dollar bill in front of the Dakota Apartments.

"Can I hold it?" she asked.

I retrieved the bill from a special place in my bag and placed it in her hand.

"It's warm," she said, "and heavy . . . a good heavy. And it's fuzzy."

"Warm and fuzzy," I said. "I like that." The young teen giggled.

"Why is it a one-dollar bill, do you think?" I asked.

"Well, it could have been a five or a ten, but it's a one. It's like you and John have one chance to do something together in this lifetime."

In my skeptical years, I doubted John Lennon's obvious spirit communication, because he was famous. It was discrimination, and it was wrong. John Baron has guided me on a thirty-year spiritual journey, yet when Lennon's personality came through, I would turn away.

My first psychic reading in the 1980s was so accurate that I shared the exciting details with a friend. She said the psychic must have checked me out beforehand, digging up details of my life so that when she gave the reading I would be astounded by her "psychic abilities."

I laughed. I was a skeptic too, yet this was ridiculous. But who was I to scoff at her doubting attitude? For three decades the spirit of John Lennon had shown himself and I doubted, asking how the spirit of a deceased Beatle could contact me. And why would he want to, I would ask cynically. And one summer, when my doubts were causing a beautiful love to die, and when I finally accepted his presence, I *still* took two steps backward. What a fool I've been.

Arriving home from New York, I unpacked a souvenir T-shirt with John Lennon's image on it and noticed the shirt's label: *Next Level*. I thought of the neon theater sign, *Leap of Faith*, and felt uneasy. I didn't want a next level or a leap of faith. Where was this going?

Four

A WEEK LATER, I sent an email to a friend (Christine Patterson), telling her about our New York trip and recalling the "love" and "leap of faith" message from John back in 2009. I shared how I had seen the *Leap of Faith* neon sign in New York.

"It's so interesting" Christine replied, "when I re-read the quote, 'Love . . . Leap . . . Leap of Faith,' my first reaction is that the big *L* is Love, and it will take you a leap of faith beyond the physical world to accepting in your heart that your love for John Baron is eternal, and that even a subsequent incarnation of John Lennon has been trying to give you affirmation to make it real to you. If you had designed it yourself, you couldn't have scripted a more cryptic neon sign than *St. James* . . . Leap of Faith. May I suggest that had John Lennon been anyone other than John Lennon, it may have been easier to accept the synchronicity of all that has happened. We all have issues of feeling unworthy in some way or another, making it especially challenging when the someone calling us to open up to the power of eternal love is an icon of our era."

Christine had hit at the heart of the matter. *Of course* I felt unworthy. I've always felt that if this had to happen—a debilitating grief over a stranger's death—why couldn't he at least have been a neighbor? It was a childish feeling, but for years that's how I felt.

Shortly after arriving at Jack and Renee's home, a bulky padded envelope came through the mail slot with a thump. I swore the envelope's address said:

Jewelle St. James

c/o the Brontës

Crikey, as the English would say, *I need new glasses!*

Jack and Renee's surname (Brodie) resembles the name Brontë, so my eyes were naturally playing tricks, I concluded.

After Renee's passing, Jack sought confirmation that his wife's spirit was still by his side. His daughter Fiona knew of a well-known psychic medium and made an appointment for her father. Perhaps Renee (in spirit) could assure Jack that she was still by his side.

Upon their return from this visit, Jack shoved a cassette tape in my direction and said, "It was a waste of money. You can listen to it, if you like."

I popped the tape into a recorder and was all ears as I listened to Jack explaining to the psychic that he wanted only one question answered: what color was Renee's engagement ring? (If the psychic could name the unique color of the engagement ring's stone, then Jack would be assured that his wife was with him.)

The psychic began describing a woman from the

seventeenth century, with beautiful hair and a long flowing dress that swept the floor. Suddenly a spirit's energy entered the picture.

"I have someone here," the psychic said, "and he would like to speak with you."

"He?" Jack sounded disappointed.

"His name is John," the psychic replied.

"I don't know anyone named John."

"John is very upset," the psychic said. "Are you sure you don't know anyone named John?"

Jack's irritation seemed to accentuate his British accent. "I don't know a John, and I don't *care* to know him."

In a gentle voice the psychic continued, "John says he was your son from another lifetime. He's very emotional. He needs to speak with you."

"Look, I'm not interested in John or anything he has to say, or a woman from the seventeenth century. I don't know these people. I came here for one reason *only*—for verification of my wife's presence by [your] naming the color of her engagement ring. Can you tell me the color or not?"

Apparently not, for the session ended abruptly.

Jack's psychic reading troubled me. The spirit who called himself John had been ignored and left hanging. Was it a coincidence that the spirit who interrupted Jack's reading just happened to be named John?

In my past experience, John had interrupted my own psychic readings. Once when I was speaking telepathically with my departed sister Konni, her first words were, *John's here and wants to use your pen*. After stating that he wanted to share information, he warned (by thought form) that I *may not be able to handle* his message.

In my head, I argued. *You can't tell me you have something to say and then wonder if I can handle it. That's not fair. Why did you bring the subject up at all?*

With a sudden jolt of my pen, and in less than two minutes, a haunting poem about the Holocaust spewed forth, containing facts (unknown to me) about the Nazi death camps in World War II. The poem ultimately took me on a journey to my last life, ending in Auschwitz, Poland.

So when a spirit named John took over Jack's reading,

it felt familiar, for I knew how Spirit-John would inter-rupt psychic readings when he "needed to speak."

The angst in the psychic's voice—telling Jack that the spirit "John" was his past-life son, who needed to speak with his past-life father—reminded me of the pain I heard in John Lennon's voice as he sang "Mother," and "Julia," spilling his pain about the loss of his mother. Or was the similarity just my imagination?

John Winston Lennon was born on October 9, 1940, in Oxford Maternity Hospital in Liverpool, England. During his childhood, he rarely saw his seaman father, (Alfred) Freddie Lennon. His mother, Julia, had a diffi-cult time trying to raise her son alone while Freddie was always away. Therefore, Julia's married sister, Mimi, took over the raising of John.

In John's early school years he was often naughty—his behavior probably the result of losing both his par-ents. Losing his mother affected John for his whole life, and perhaps his second wife, Yoko Ono, who was older than John, was a mother figure for him. John's endearing nickname for Yoko was "Mother."

In John's teen years, he and Julia were becoming reacquainted. One afternoon as Julia was crossing the street near Mimi's house, she was struck and killed by a car. John would later say he felt he'd lost his mother twice in his lifetime.

ANN ARBOR, MI — Dec 10: Musician John Lennon formerly of 'The Beatles' performs onstage at the Chrysler Arena on Dec 10, 1971 in Ann Arbor, Michigan. (Photo by Tom Copi / Michael Ochs Archive/ Getty Images)

Five

BACK IN THE LATE 1980s, my full attention was on seventeenth-century Sussex, England. One night while watching an English TV show, a scene of green countryside with rolling hills dotted with centuries-old stone fences struck my heart like a physical attack, and I wanted to cry: *I want to go home.*

The ending credits showed that the program had been produced by Yorkshire Television Production. Back then, my knowledge of England was limited, yet I knew that Yorkshire was in the north and Sussex was in the south. I couldn't understand this overwhelming wave of homesickness for northern England, a swift, longing feeling that made no logical sense.

Only now do I see and accept, through decades of searching for John and Katherine's past, a parallel story has been begging for attention: the possible reincarnation connections between John Lennon and the Brontës.

Long ago, a cousin commented that our family's isolated life in the wilds of nature resembled that of the Brontës from nineteenth-century England. I'd never heard of the literary family, yet vaguely recalled reading *Jane Eyre* by Charlotte Brontë, so now, out of curiosity, I picked up a biography about Emily Brontë.

Through my teen years we lived in the heart of the Canadian Rocky Mountains in Yoho National Park. There were more elk and bears than people in our remote area, yet I couldn't see or feel any connection with an English family living more than one hundred years earlier, except perhaps our shared isolation.

In the late 1980s I joined a genealogy group whose members helped me find Katherine's birth records, and where I met a new friend, Herma. Herma and I discovered a common interest other than genealogy—spirituality and Herma's budding psychic abilities.

We did a few psychic tests, fooling around, really, and I asked Herma if she could guess my past-life name; I wondered if she could conjure up Katherine. Herma called an hour later. Although our conversation took place many years ago, my memory of it remains vivid.

"Did you get a past-life name for me?" I asked, expecting Katherine.

"No, not a name, only initials," Herma said.

Anticipating *K* or *C,* Herma announced, *"E."* Before I could question her further, she added, "Actually, it was *E.B."*

"E.B.?" I repeated, hoping to hide my disappointment.

"Yes." Herma's voice was confident. *"E.B.* is connected to you in some way."

Herma must have ESP, I decided, for just that day I had been reading a biography about Emily Brontë. *E.B.*

I decided to test Herma further, and that night drove to her house with the Emily Brontë biography tucked in my bag. I had used masking tape to hide all identifying words on the book cover, leaving only Emily's portrait visible. I didn't know at the time that it would be a night to remember.

Herma's home, tucked amongst trees at the end of a driveway, was a calm refuge from a busy world. We sat on overstuffed couches, sipping chamomile tea.

"Herma, I want to show you something." I reached in my bag for Emily's biography. "I'm going to show you a portrait of a lady—just tell me whatever comes to mind, okay?"

Herma nodded.

I held up the book covered in masking tape, revealing only Emily Brontë's image. Five seconds passed before Herma blurted, "John Lennon was her brother."

"What?" I exclaimed.

"In another life of John Lennon's, he had been this lady's brother."

I called my sister Konni the next day. "Are you going to check it out?" she asked.

"What's to check out? Herma and I were just fooling

around. It all started when I asked her if she'd like to test her psychic abilities."

"Tell me this," Konni said, "did Emily Brontë have a brother?"

"Yes, his name was Branwell."

"Don't you think it odd that John's name popped up, even when you were fooling around?"

"I guess so," I mumbled.

"Do me a favor, okay? Just for fun. Go see whatever similarities there are between John Lennon and Branwell Brontë."

Knowing it would be much easier to research than to argue with my sister, I promised to report back. I called Konni a week later. Her hunch was correct. There *were* similarities between the two men, and through the years even more parallels between Lennon and Brontë have been revealed.

In addition to Branwell and John looking almost identical, similar details of their lives came to light:

~ both suffered from myopia (short-sightedness)

~ both were raised surrounded by females

~ each lost his mother to an early death

~ each was raised by a childless aunt, an elder sister of each boy's mother: Mary Elizabeth ("Mimi") for Lennon and Elizabeth for Brontë

~ both boys were born and raised in northern England

~ their fathers' ancestors came from County Down, Ireland

~ from childhood each boy considered himself a genius

~ at an early age both had equal creative talents and vocations—art student and poet—and they both loved music

~ in their boyhood and adolescent years both handcrafted their own books, newspapers, and magazines

~ both wrote, doodled, and scribbled their entire lives

~ both were known for their sardonic humor

~ each struggled with drug addictions and alcohol abuse

~ both were fond of using pseudonyms (Branwell's favorite was *Northangerland*, while John Lennon called himself *Dr. Winston O'Boogie*)

~ the surnames Lennon and Brontë have identical numerology

~ they share some identical astrological aspects (Branwell Brontë and John Lennon's astrology are explored in *The Hades Moon* by Judy Hall.)

Seven years after Herma's surprising announcement about John Lennon and Emily Brontë's brother being the same soul, a friend sent me a magazine article about a psychic who apparently had channeled the spirit of John Lennon in the early 1980s. Eventually I connected with the psychic. I didn't mention the Brontës to her—it didn't cross my mind to do so—so I was shocked when she said that, according to her channeled messages, Emily Brontë was John's favorite poet. I didn't mention Herma's sense that Branwell Brontë was the same soul as John Lennon, so I nearly fainted when the psychic later stated that Branwell Brontë was a former lifetime of John Lennon's.

In our conversations I wondered out loud whether I had "made the past lives [of John and Katherine] up in my head," doubts that had always plagued me. In a letter the psychic replied, "Jewelle, I've tuned into John's spirit to ask what he thinks of John and Katherine's life together in Petworth. This is the response I get:

The answer is to accept that what Spirit has informed you is correct. Your lives were as stated, don't question facts. John and Katherine, the music, the dancing, all belong to that life together. As do John and Emily Brontë."

The psychic continued, "John and Emily Brontë. The answer is a simple one. In one of John's past lives he was Branwell Brontë. This is the reason he brought Emily into your life and mine."

In 1994 I went to England and was thrilled when my brother and his wife, who lived in the English Midlands, took me to Yorkshire. The trip included a visit to the Brontës' home in Haworth.

A cool wind blew as we climbed the steep main street of Haworth, past Branwell's favorite watering hole, the Black Bull Pub, to the Brontës' home, The Parsonage. Now a museum, The Parsonage is a two-story stone house hugging the moors at the back and overlooking a bleak cemetery at the front.

I followed a group of tourists from room to room. As we went into the kitchen, a thought entered my head from out of the blue: *This is wrong. The kitchen is wrong.* Seconds later, I saw a sign on the wall stating that the kitchen had been renovated since the Brontës had lived here. It was a moment of knowing I can't explain.

The Brontë Parsonage, Haworth, Yorkshire.

Upon leaving The Parsonage museum, I was *dying* to walk out on the moors, but my sister-in-law was shaking with cold, and who could blame her in the raw weather, so I kept silent.

Years later I asked a friend if she thought the Brontë-kitchen incident had been a "psychic fluke," and she said it was more like a "knowing."

Nearly twenty years after the Brontë-kitchen incident, on a cool, blustery spring morning, another "kitchen incident" occurred. Spirit-John announced he had a message and would deliver it that day through Jack.

All morning I hung on to Jack's every word, but nothing seemed like a message, and by noon I'd forgotten about it.

In the mid-afternoon, Jack came in from the outside. He shed his coat while leaving a huge scarf wrapped around his neck and stood at the kitchen sink, replacing a water filter. When he put on his glasses to examine his project, I nearly fainted.

While on a return visit to Haworth (in 2010), I'd had a good look at the Reverend Brontë's portrait at The Parsonage, and now the same image stood only three feet away. I hung on to the kitchen counter, staring at Jack, feeling as if I'd entered another time and place.

Jack doesn't usually wear his glasses, but that day he did. A large scarf, draped from chin to chest, was the exact replica of the large white silk scarf that Patrick Brontë became known for wearing every day of his adult life. But it was his face. I'd never observed Jack's face closely from a side view.

Today, in a surreal moment, truth stared me in the face, and everything changed. Something made me look at the calendar. It was St. Patrick's Day, Reverend Patrick Brontë's birthday (born in Ireland on March 17, 1777.)

That night I recalled John's telepathic words from the morning, saying he would send a message through Jack, and there it was: Jack was the reincarnation of Reverend Patrick Brontë. Or that was my interpretation. John/Branwell *was* the son who "needed to speak" (through Jack's psychic reading) with his past-life father!

After Jack's daughter Fiona had completed the design and typesetting of *All You Need Is Love* in 2009, she surprised me with a job offer to care for her parents. On the day of the interview, fear suddenly dictated that moving across British Columbia to a new home and job wasn't a good idea.

I flew to Vancouver and met Jack and Renee for a casual job interview at their home. They were a lovely couple, yet I wanted to bolt out the door, probably fearing the unknown. Just then a loud "thought form," seemingly from the top of Renee's head, boomed: *Come.*

Weeks later, Renee and I sat in their beautiful English garden, and we laughed about the silent yet deafening "voice" that had demanded I obey and take the job and live with the English couple in their home.

Now, after seeing "Papa Brontë" standing in the kitchen, I had to wonder: Had I been sent here because Jack is Branwell/John's past life father? *But why?*

Six

PATRICK BRONTË WAS born into a poor family, the eldest of ten children, in County Down, Ireland. He was self-taught, becoming a teacher before he left Ireland and enrolled at St. John's College in Cambridge, England, studying theology.

Jack didn't attend university until after his retirement. For seven years, after the age of sixty, he attended a university in Vancouver—the idea was to keep his brain sharp while satisfying his life-long thirst for knowledge.

**Author John J. Ross, M.D., described the Reverend Brontë: "Patrick was a man of keen intelligence and unusual drive." No better words could describe Jack.

The Reverend Brontë was also a polemist: a debater, an arguer. I had to smile on learning that. To put it mildly, Jack thrives on a good "discussion."

Upon moving to England and entering college, Patrick changed his surname from Brunty to Brontë. Jack changed his Christian given name, selecting "Jack," because he disliked his legal name.

Patrick was the first Brontë to pen books, although none became popular. Jack wrote his autobiography—not that you'll see it on any bestseller's book list, he quips, as only four copies were printed.

Both men left their native lands for a better life. Patrick left Ireland and moved to England, and Jack left England and came to Canada.

Both were Tories, seriously absorbed in all current politics of the day. Both were avid champions of protecting our environment. Reverend Brontë lobbied for a clean water supply for the village of Haworth.

The similarities between the two men were interesting, but nothing like "seeing" Papa Brontë/Jack in the kitchen that day.

Upon moving to Jack and Renee's home, the coincidences between their lives and mine were uncanny, considering we had met by fate. Not only was the family from West Sussex, near Katherine's past-life home, but the whole family were all about books.

Renee wrote two popular metaphysical books, Fiona is a book designer and soon-to-be author, while Jack acquired the role of book publisher. Jack's son recently wrote his first book. (Through the writing of this book, Jack's son and daughter were both writing their own—three of us writing books at once.)

Even my new living quarters had once been a storage area for all the materials a self-publisher would need to operate a business. For so long I had lived in a world where few related to my love of "making books," and now I was in a place where spirituality and books were a way of life.

Upon first arriving in Little England and becoming acquainted with Jack and Renee, there was no lack of conversational topics. We discussed books, editors, shipping methods, printers, and distribution. Then there was the topic of Sussex, England. Jack knew every turn and road in West Sussex—a certain pub in Midhurst or the stone wall running parallel to dark North Street in Petworth—and it was as if I'd known the family forever.

It was hard wrapping my head around Jack being the reincarnation of the Reverend Brontë, although I "knew" it was he who stood in the kitchen that day. I asked Jack if he was familiar with Yorkshire. He'd driven through the northern counties when stationed in Scotland with the RAF, but had had no reason to stop in wild Yorkshire, he said. Jack was clearly a "southern" Englishman from Chichester, proud of his Sussex roots, and seemed to have no interest in the north. (Later a friend said that of course he avoided Yorkshire, for if he'd once been the Reverend Brontë, he had lost everyone he ever loved there.)

My spiritual journey required, or so I felt, that I return to the Brontës' home in Haworth, Yorkshire. When Spirit-John had told me to get re-acquainted with the Brontës, I'd felt it was perhaps because Branwell Brontë and John Lennon were the same soul. The only way to unearth more information was to return to Branwell's home.

Emily seemed an unfortunate connection in my quest, yet I had a simple solution: I would "shut her out" while visiting the Brontës' home. I would be there for Branwell. I didn't want to "be" Emily, investigate her, or even think about her.

In November 2010, I flew from Vancouver to London. After resting in Sussex for a weekend, I took the long journey by train from London to medieval York and on to Haworth. I had felt, months before the trip, that Spirit-John would be my "tour guide," and indeed he was present from beginning to end.

My train trip ended at Keighley, an old industrial town near Haworth. Blackened stone houses lined the three-mile journey from Keighley to Haworth, up a long, meandering hill with stunning views of the moors. My B&B was in the center of Haworth, steps away from the Brontës' home/museum, The Parsonage, in one direction and a stone's throw from "Branwell's pub," the Black Bull, in the other direction.

The view from my bedroom window reminded me of the Yorkshire TV series *Heartbeat*. I wasted no time unpacking, headed up the cobblestoned lane, past the church and cemetery that seemed to spill into the Brontës' front garden, and up the steps to the stone building that had once been Branwell's family home.

The tour of The Parsonage began with the Reverend Patrick Brontë's study. A portrait of him as a young man hangs on the wall—eerily, his eyes are identical to John Lennon's.

By luck and coincidence, the Brontë Parsonage Museum was featuring an exhibition: Sex, Drugs and Literature— The Infernal Life of Branwell Brontë.

Portrait of Reverend Patrick Brontë as a young man.
'Courtesy of The Brontë Society.'

The exhibition told the story of Branwell, from the young boy's beginnings as the beloved family genius (he was the first Brontë to have poetry published in newspapers) to the troubled, unhappy young adult.

A museum steward said, "Branwell excelled at carica-
tures but never seriously pursued that route." Observing
his sophisticated drawings, I felt it was a shame that one
so brilliantly talented had not reached his full potential.

I spent most of every day in Haworth at The Parsonage. Strangely, I longed to stay at the Brontës' home and
felt cheated having to return to the B&B each night.

My arrival coincided with the publication of Dr. Juliet
Barker's biography, *The Brontës* (2010) and I was thrilled
to purchase a copy from the museum's bookstore.

One stormy afternoon I returned to my room to read
Dr. Barker's excellent new book. I had a strange feeling, reading about the Brontës while being yards from
their home.

Dr. Barker wrote that Branwell, in 1840, had possibly fathered a child by one of three servant girls when
employed as a tutor in the Lake District. One maid was
named Eleanor Nelson. My maternal grandmother's name
is Eleanor Nelson! I've never known anyone with my
grandmother's name, so it was a surprising coincidence.

The wind rattled the B&B's windows, and my thoughts came back to Branwell's child. No infants of the various servant girls survived, so no direct Brontë family line was continued.

In 2005, however, a Yorkshire newspaper (*The Huddersfield Daily Examiner*) reported a story about a Mirfield woman, Mrs. Imelda Marsden, who re-published a biography about the Reverend Brontë: *The Father of the Brontës* (*1897*) by W W Yates. Mrs. Marsden, a remarkable researcher, also unearthed the history of a Brontë relative—Rose Ann Heslip. Rose Ann, the daughter of Patrick Brontë's sister Sarah, had moved from Ireland to Yorkshire. Mrs. Marsden undertook a search for Rose Ann's descendants and found her great-granddaughter back in Ireland whose surname is Lennon.

Seven

Jane Eyre or *Wuthering Heights* would not have been written if the Brontë family had lived in London or Paris. Authors write about what they know, and the Brontës knew a harsh world in a remote little village called Haworth in the west riding of Yorkshire. Their parsonage home, at the top of the village's main street, was a stone building provided by the parish for the Reverend and his family.

Haworth's main street was so steep that it had been cobbled to assist a horse and cart in the climb. The Parsonage overlooked the church and cemetery at its front, while vast barren moors began at their back door.

After studying theology at St. John's College, Cambridge, Patrick (in 1806) became the Reverend Patrick Brontë. In 1812 he met his wife, Maria Branwell, from gentle Cornwell, and they started their married life in West Yorkshire where Patrick held various posts.

After their two eldest daughters, Maria and Elizabeth, were born in Hartshead, Yorkshire, they moved to Thornton, Yorkshire, where the Reverend Brontë was curate at St. James Church, and where the next four Brontës were born: Charlotte (1816), Patrick Branwell (known as Branwell), named after his mother's maiden name (1817), Emily Jane (1818), and Anne (1820.)

Little Anne was still a baby when the Reverend Brontë left his post in Thornton, and the young family moved to Haworth to their father's new position. Here they would spend the rest of their lives.

About eighteen months after their arrival in Haworth, Patrick's wife died of cancer, leaving her husband and little ones alone in the stone parsonage.

Luckily for Patrick, Maria's unmarried sister (Elizabeth Branwell), who had traveled from Penzance, Cornwall,

to care for her sister, remained to help raise her brother-
in-law's six little motherless children, all under the age of
seven. Neither Aunt Branwell nor the Reverend Brontë had
an understanding of little children's needs. Therefore the
little Brontës turned to each other for comfort and love.

A. Mary F. Robinson wrote (*Emily Brontë 1883*):

After his wife's death the Rev. Mr. Brontë's
life grew yet more secluded from ordinary human
interests. He was not intimate with his parishio-
ners; scarcely more intimate with his children. He
was proud of when they said anything clever, for, in
spite of their babyhood, he felt at such moments that
they were worthy of their father; but their forlorn
infancy, their helpless ignorance, was no appeal to
his heart. Some months before his wife's death he
had begun to take his dinner alone, on account of
his delicate digestion; and he continued the habit,
seeing the children seldom except at breakfast and
tea, when he would amuse the elders by talking Tory
politics with them, and entertain the baby, Emily,

with his Irish tales of violence and horror. Perhaps on account of this very aloofness, he always had a great influence over the children; he did not care for any dearer relation.

His empty days were filled with occasional visits to some sick person in the village; with long walks alone over the moors, and with the composition of his "Cottage in the Wood" and those grandiloquent sermons which still linger in the memory of Haworth. Occasionally a clergyman from one of the neighbouring villages would walk over to see him; but as Mrs. Brontë had died so soon after her arrival at Haworth their wives never came, and the Brontë children had no playfellows in the vicarages near; nor were they allowed to associate with the village children.

Meanwhile the children were left alone. For sympathy and amusement they only had each other to look to; and never were brother and sisters more devoted. Maria, the eldest, took care of them all— she was an old fashioned, motherly little girl; frail and small in appearance, with thoughtful, tender ways. She was very careful of her five little ones, this seven year old mother of theirs, and never seems to have exerted the somewhat tyrannic authority usually wielded by such youthful guardians. Indeed, for all her seniority, she was the untidy one of the family herself; it was against her own faults only that she was severe. She must have been a very attaching little creature, with her childish delinquencies and her womanly cares; protecting her little family with gentle love and discussing the debates in Parliament with her father. Charlotte remembered her to the end of her life with passionate clinging affection and has left us her portrait in the pathetic figure of Helen Burns (in *Jane Eyre.*)

This delicate, weak chested, child of seven was the head of the nursery. Then came Elizabeth, less clearly individualised in her sisters' memory. She also bore in her tiny body the seed of fatal consumption. Next came impetuous Charlotte, always small and pale. Then red-headed, talkative Patrick Branwell.

Lastly Emily and Anne, mere babies, toddling with difficulty over the paven path to the moors.

In 1824 Patrick Brontë had the opportunity to have his four eldest daughters (Maria, Elizabeth, Charlotte, and Emily) sent to a boarding school for "daughters of poor clergy" and educated at a reasonable cost—a move that caused the family a (forever devastating) loss.

The new school—the Clergy Daughter's School in Cowan Bridge, about forty miles from Haworth—was opened by a Lancashire clergyman, Reverend William Carus Wilson. At this time Branwell was educated at home by his father, and little Anne was only four years old. In later years, in Charlotte Brontë's brilliant *Jane Eyre,* Reverend Wilson, the headmaster of the Cowan Bridge boarding school, was depicted as the cruel Mr. Brockle-hurst, while Charlotte's elder sister Maria was the saintly Helen Burns. (It's strange—Reverend Carus Wilson's portrait is the exact image of someone I know.)

The school's severe environment—no proper heat, inedible food, no love or compassion, and an abusive "hell and damnation" religion that terrorized "naughty children"—resulted in the deaths of Maria and Elizabeth Brontë, who died (of consumption) within one month of each other at ages eleven and ten.

Both girls are buried in Haworth. Little Maria, who was treated so badly at the boarding school, had been a loving mother figure to her siblings after their own mother, also named Maria, had died. She was a true little saint.

After the deaths of Maria and Elizabeth, Reverend Brontë immediately brought Charlotte and Emily home from Cowan Bridge boarding school.

For the next four years, Charlotte, Branwell, Emily, and Anne were home-schooled by their aunt and father.

Francis A. Leyland (brother of Branwell's best friend, J.B. Leyland) wrote in *The Brontë Family, with special reference to Patrick Branwell Brontë* (1886):

Upon the return of Charlotte and Emily from Cowan Bridge, the youthful Brontës, whom death had spared, were united again; and, for some years more, followed their pursuits together, until Charlotte went to school at Roe Head in 1831. Branwell was the constant companion of his sisters during these childish years, and they all looked upon him with pride and affection. Charlotte, in those days, was a sympathetic friend to him; and, in his later years, he felt a source of deep regret that she was somewhat estranged. But the gentle Emily—after the death of Maria—was his chief companion, and a warm affection never lost its ardour between them.

Leyland described the Brontës' young years:

The childhood of the Brontës in the parsonage of Haworth has been pictured to us as a very strange one indeed. We have seen them deprived in their early youth of maternal care which they required so much, and left in the hands of a father unfamiliar with such a charge, who was filled with Spartan ideas of discipline, and theories of education above and beyond the capacity of childhood. There was probably little room in the house for gaiety and amusement, very little tolerance for pretty dress, or home beauty, and small comprehension of child-ish needs. Rigid formality, silent chambers, staid attire, frugal fare, and secluded lives fell to the lot of these thoughtful and gifted children. It was no wonder that they grew up "grave and silent beyond their years."

Eight

SHORTLY BEFORE Branwell's ninth birthday in June, 1826, the children's lives changed forever when Patrick brought home a set of wooden soldiers. The children fell upon the small soldiers as if every thirsty bone in their psyches had been waiting for an outlet for their budding creativity.

The four children assigned each soldier a character's name from their own heroes about whom they'd read in their father's weekly magazines and newspapers of the day. Soon Charlotte, Branwell, Emily, and Anne were creating imaginary kingdoms centered around these life-like wooden soldiers. Charlotte and Branwell created a world called Glass Town and "published" numerous self-made miniature books; Glass Town then evolved into an imaginary land that Charlotte and Branwell called Angria.

The soldiers were brought to life as the children invented worlds told through stories, plays, and magazines, and they wrote manuscripts that were lovingly made into miniature books.

Eventually the younger children, Emily and Anne, created their own imaginary world, Gondal. Emily, of all the Brontë children, never abandoned her "inner" world and took her imagined creations with her into adulthood.

When Emily was in her late twenties, she and Anne took their first trip alone to visit historic York. The world of Gondal went with them. In Emily's diary she later wrote of their trip only in reference to their inner world of Gondal characters, not mentioning the outer world—the beauty of York Minster, the ancient streets, or the history of the city. Emily's outer world could never compete with her rich inner world, not even on a visit with Anne to beautiful York.

Emily and her siblings retained their father's Irish accent—another oddity setting them apart from others. Emily was painfully shy, she never learned social skills, was aloof with strangers, appearing to most as rude, and if confronted by any person outside her family circle, she would avert her eyes and not utter a word. She was a loner who loved nature and animals more than people.

Like all the Brontës, Emily left home on occasion, once studying in a boarding school in Brussels with Charlotte (their unsuccessful plan was to become fully educated and open a girls' school in Haworth).

While in Brussels they socialized somewhat; Charlotte was social, while Emily was disliked by nearly everyone for her cold, aloof attitude, and soon all social invitations stopped.

Emily, who wore clothing long out of fashion, was mocked by the other students for her lack of style. She would reply, "I wish to be as God made me."

Biographer Romer Wilson wrote in *All Alone: The Life and Private History of Emily Jane Brontë* (1928):

". . . in February, 1842, Old Brontë dug himself out of the Parsonage and took his two pale-faced daughters aged twenty-five and twenty-three to school there, to sleep and eat and learn with children on an average ten years younger. Charlotte, according to French ideas and doubtless Belgian, had already entered upon the vocation of Old Maid. Emily, gaunt and sallow and masculine, must have seemed to the cheerful fat daughters of Brussels a veritable amphibian out of water."

Charlotte understood Emily's behaviour—Emily could not function in the outside world.

While Charlotte and Emily studied in Brussels, Aunt Elizabeth Branwell died (once more Branwell felt he'd lost a mother) and the girls quickly returned home to Haworth, and later only Charlotte returned to school.

Charlotte was secretly in love with her Brussels professor (but that's another story), and Emily chose to remain at home.

Another time and place—Emily was a student while

Charlotte was a teacher at the same school called Roe Head—and where soon Emily, severely home-sick, needed to return to Haworth, or literally perish. Indeed, there was no place that Emily could survive away from the moors and the Parsonage.

Luckily for Emily, after their Aunt Elizabeth Branwell died, the Brontë sisters each received a small inheritance, large enough to keep Emily forever at home. Branwell did not inherit from his aunt, as she assumed (as did the whole family) that the talented Branwell would be a financial success, providing for them all in their later years.

I began telling Jack a bit about the Reverend Brontë. Many stories abound concerning the Brontë family, some true, no doubt, while others are probably village gossip:

Patrick was said to have sawed off the backs of all the kitchen chairs. Jack didn't skip a beat: "The children soon learned to sit up straight, didn't they?"

I told Jack how the children clung together after their

mother's death, Mrs. Brontë having died of cancer after giving birth to six children within seven years of marriage. Jack's demeanor changed, and for about twenty minutes he (strangely) railed against the Reverend Brontë, although he knew little about the man. Jack said the Reverend should have given his wife some breathing room, and that having six children in seven years was unacceptable.

"He was a selfish man," he muttered.

According to Romer Wilson, "In a sense Emily and Branwell were mad and Charlotte intermittently mad."

"Well, no surprise," Jack insisted. "The Brontë father drove them crazy by his lack of love and his strict ways. No wonder the children suffered. Brontë was a hard, stubborn, self-centered man."

Months later, one sun-filled morning, it struck me that John/Branwell needed to speak with his "father," and since Jack hadn't allowed the John-spirit to "speak" through the psychic reading, I would have to relay Branwell's message myself, if indeed it *was* Branwell's message.

Jack was nobody's fool. He'd been raised in Sussex, England, by Victorian parents in a military family and did service in the Royal Air Force during World War II. He later studied at the London College of Music and was an aircraft inspector. This impressive list went on, and that was before he moved to Canada, embarking on another successful career.

So here I was, about to tell this man of the world that John Lennon had been his son in a former life, and that his "son" had a message to relay! It was one thing to discuss hypothetical scenarios with Jack about the Brontës, but this was over the top.

And anyway, how would I bring up the subject?

But in *less than ten minutes* after coming up with my ludicrous plan to relay the message, Jack brought up the subject himself by ranting about that "charlatan psychic reader" who couldn't answer his question concerning his wife's engagement ring.

I honestly couldn't believe my ears. It had been weeks

since Jack had mentioned his "so-called psychic reading." He vowed that he'd never pay good money again to be ripped off by a woman who, instead of tuning into his departed wife, started speaking nonsense from a spirit named George.

"His name was John," I said quietly.

"John, George, whoever, he's nobody to me!"

I was stunned. The opportunity was there, but did I have a clue what I was talking about, relaying a message to Jack from John/Branwell? Yet something or someone urged me on, for the timing was now or never.

"Jack," I began, "there's something about that psychic reading . . . the emotional spirit named John, who 'came through,' the one who said he was your past-life son . . . well, I suspect I know who that spirit is, and I possibly know the message he wants to relay. Jack, please hear me out, okay?"

"Fine," Jack said.

I took a deep breath. "Jack, I believe you are the reincarnated father of the Brontës, the Reverend Patrick Brontë. I know it sounds outrageous, but that's why the spirit in your psychic reading said you were his past-life father and stated his name was John. John was once your son, Branwell Brontë. Are you with me, Jack, do you understand what I'm saying?"

"Yes."

"John/Branwell is upset because he needs you to know he is deeply sorry. He was a terrible son, putting his father through hell, drinking, addicted to drugs, spending everyone's money, being a complete disappointment. He knows he messed up his life, but more so, he let his family down. He let *you* down."

"Then why didn't he do something about it?" Jack seemed angry. "Why carry on in that manner if he knew better?"

I fought tears. "Branwell couldn't help himself. He was young and an alcoholic, and he died before he could get his act together. He knows he was a failure. He needs your forgiveness."

God, this is crazy, I thought.

"Jack," I said, "do you understand what I'm saying?"

"Yes," he replied.

He seemed agitated, but said he understood the message.

It was surreal how Jack stayed with me throughout our conversation, and I felt he truly *did* get it, never wavering from John/Branwell's message, never acting like this conversation was insane.

And we have never discussed this again.

Nine

OVER A SPAN of twenty-five years, I have purchased several copies of *Wuthering Heights* (1847) by Emily Brontë, yet I cannot read the book. I have tried. The various movie versions of the book are first-rate, and there are no dull moments, but I watch with more of a technical eye rather than embracing the turbulent, wild, passionate love story of Heathcliff and Catherine roaming the Yorkshire moors in their inclusive, self-centered world.

Over the decades, when I'm on my questing trips to England, *Wuthering Heights* nearly always plays on TV within days of my departure or on my return. It took several trips to see this pattern. While I was on the flight home from my last trip to England in 2010, a friend left a phone message saying *Wuthering Heights* was playing on TV.

Last year I received a copy of *Wuthering Heights* for Christmas, yet after a few chapters, I had to stop reading.

Long ago, a psychic said that Emily and Branwell's manuscripts "are buried together." I thought the idea was far-fetched and visualized moldy, tattered papers buried under a tree somewhere on the barren, wind-swept Yorkshire moors. But what if they *are* buried together?

One of Jack's studies after his retirement was psychology. I wondered if he could analyze my inability to read *Wuthering Heights*.

"Jack, let's just hypothesize," I began, "that in a past life I was Emily Brontë, the author of *Wuthering Heights*. Some say that her brother, Branwell, had a hand in writing the book. Others say he wrote the whole book. Either way, why can't I read it? I love watching the movie, yet reading the book's words and sentences is impossible."

Jack stated flatly, "Guilty conscience. The words aren't *your* words, and you feel guilty. That's why you turn away from the book, yet it still keeps nagging at you."

Really? But somehow it made sense.

I began reading Brontë biographies from writers in the 1800s who knew Branwell personally or who had privy to his friends' memories.

Charlotte's friend, and biographer, Mrs. Elizabeth Gaskell wrote the first Brontë biography: *The Life of Charlotte Brontë (1857.)*

There's a theory (floating around since the nineteenth century) that Branwell Brontë, the genius yet wayward brother, wrote all or part of *Wuthering Heights* (although most Brontë biographers refute the idea.)

After plowing through a number of different opinions—Victorian-era authors claiming that Emily Brontë had the assistance of her brother's hand in writing *Wuthering Heights*, or that Branwell was *the* genius behind all his sisters' works, or that he was simply a hindrance to their lives in general —I slowly formed my own opinion, based more on a *feeling* than anyone else's opinion. The true authorship of *Wuthering Heights*, that most would call a non-issue, caused an uneasiness within me.

I threw my opinion into the mix and agreed (in part) with author Alice Law, who not only defended Branwell's reputation (bless her), but stated that indeed, he had had his hand in Emily's novel. Law wrote (in *Patrick Branwell Brontë*, 1923):

> In common with many other dwellers on the borders of the West Riding of Yorkshire, within a radius of some twenty odd miles from Haworth, I was brought up in the Brontë atmosphere. I have paid many visits to the little grey parsonage on the sky-line of the gaunt uplands, and every pilgrimage has intensified my profound pity for the unhappy life and blighted ambitions of Patrick Branwell Brontë, a feeling even predominating over my admiration for the genius of his sisters. This feeling might have remained pity, and nothing more, had it not been at length roused to something warmer by finding such a torrent of unmitigated abuse of Charlotte's

despised brother in all the Brontë literature, both present and past, as made one suspect there must be some source of irritation against him not immediately manifest to the general public.

Yet the more I pondered over his case, the more inexplicable it became to suppose that the youth whom Mrs. Gaskell—a writer so near to the heart of things through her friendship with Charlotte—had pronounced to be "perhaps to begin with, the greatest genius in this rare family," could have passed through nearly thirty-one years of life without leaving some work of value behind him. "To begin with"—the phrase is curious. One realizes the suggestion behind it—that Branwell, both as a boy and youth, gave promise of achievements which he never performed, and that having wasted and neglected his powers, he finally lost them. This opened up the question in my mind—Can genius perish utterly in a man? Even though the vessel be wrecked, will not some spars, some precious cargo float to land to shew (sic) what a rich-laden and goodly ship has floundered? What became of Branwell's undoubted genius?

In this perplexed state of mind I came across Mr. Francis A. Leyland's book on *"The Brontë Family,"* *written with special reference to Patrick Branwell Brontë,* giving various fragments of Branwell's work, and, most important of all, quoting his declaration that he had written a great portion of *Wuthering Heights.* [Francis Leyland, like Alice Law, wrote in defense of Branwell, after Branwell's death.]

The "murder" was out, and my suspicions concerning the marked animus shewn (sic) by the biographers of the Brontës—those of Emily in particular—towards Branwell, were at once confirmed. I began to understand something of the rage and indignation such an assertion would rouse in the minds of the staunch supporters of Emily's authorship, an authorship so confidently vouched for by Charlotte. I began to realize how necessary it was for the enthusiastic partisans of Emily and Charlotte to counter what Mr. Clement Shorter terms this "preposterous statement" of Branwell's, by endeavouring to shew (sic) him up as a thoroughly unreliable wastrel and liar. Greatly impressed with Mr. Leyland's very fair and balanced account of Branwell, I determined to study the matter more closely, with the result that I am convinced there is much evidence to substantiate his claim. To dismiss it as the biographers of Emily Brontë have done, with mere derision and rancorous contempt, is futile; abuse is not an argument. It remains, therefore, in the interests of literary justice that Branwell's claim should be carefully examined, as I have endeavoured, however inadequately, to examine it in the following pages, and I venture to submit the accumulated evidence which has been brought to light since Mr. Leyland's day to the unbiased judgements of my readers.

Where no absolutely direct proof can be adduced, I have employed conjecture as, taken together with all the obvious points of the case, amounts well-nigh to certainty.

From her chapter "The Biographers," Alice Law states:

The history of the Brontë family, with one exception, that of their brother, the subject of this memoir has been so often told as to call for little further comment. The story of Patrick Branwell Brontë, on the other hand, has but cropped up incidentally in the biographies of his famous sisters, hurriedly, apologetically thrust in, to illustrate certain aspects of, or crises in their lives. The reference has been usually brief and damnatory, the pitiable narrative being introduced chiefly as a foil to display how their genius triumphed despite the stumbling block of a brother's disgrace, strewn in the path of their achievement. Mrs. Gaskell passes him with a shudder, referring to him as one who proved the bane of his sisters lives; Sir Wemyss Reid, in his monograph upon Charlotte, refers to him as "this lost and degraded man"; Miss Mary Robinson (Madame Duclaux), in her study of Emily, cannot find words sufficiently scathing to convey her contempt for Branwell; and Mr. Swinburne, in his review of Miss Robinson's work, adds his invective to hers. Within the last quarter century other writers have gone out of their way to heap contempt and obloquy upon this unfortunate young man. Mr. Clement Shorter dismisses his pretensions to genius in the harshest fashion, and Miss Sinclair, relying perhaps too much on Mr. Shorter's judgment, and for a reason which I hope to presently make plain, acquiesces in, and even emphasizes the general condemnation.

While at first generously deploring the perpetual digging up of poor Branwell, Miss Sinclair finally, in her study of "The Three Brontës," begins to dig as fast as anyone, and to drive as many nails as possible into the coffin of his reputation.

Indeed, this necessity of repudiating Branwell has become a kind of obsession among Brontë writers, so much so that they seem to fear that unless Branwell is defamed, the sisters cannot come into their full inheritance of glory.

From what we know of Charlotte, Emily and Anne Brontë, we can guess that they would owe their biographers scant thanks for such a miserable tribute to their reputation. Assuredly the lustre of their renown is brilliant enough, and needs no such deplorable foil. Yet, so it has been: from the time of Mrs. Gaskell until now, Branwell Brontë's failure has been everywhere emphasized to magnify his sisters' success or to enhance the pathos of their sufferings, until it is scarcely an exaggeration to say that his poor life and reputation have been used, much as were the bodies of some of the early Christians—tarred with obloquy and burned with a torch to throw a more lurid light on the struggles of his kinsfolk bathing in life's arena. His own martyrdom, at the hands of Fate and Family, has passed unheeded.

There is perhaps in the whole history of English literature—usually so generous to the claims of genius however handicapped by temperament or hampered by circumstance—no parallel instance of any writer of equal ability being subjected to the indiscriminate abuse heaped on Branwell Brontë. It is indeed time that all this execration should cease. Shameful if continued against the most ordinary human being, it becomes an outrage against the memory of one who had so little good fortune in his short lifetime; who died in his thirty-first year, a victim to the hereditary disease which devastated in turn the members of his family; and who left behind him fragments of art and literature which indicate the highest promise of what he might have attained in a more favourable environment.

Mr. Brontë was the first to strongly resent Mrs. Gaskell's uncalled-for attacks upon both himself and his son, and since then there have happily been a few gallant defenders of Branwell Brontë, to whose impressions the more weight may be attached since they either knew him personally or were in touch with those who did. The report they render, taken as a whole, is markedly in his favour. The other writers denouncing him, on the other hand, are those who have merely judged him from rumour and heresy. Their almost hysterical accounts against him leave the reader with the suspicion that they had some particular grudge against him, and, as I hope presently to shew, [sic] they undoubtedly have. The peevishness of these writers, makes them all, with the notable exception of Mr. Clement Shorter, strive to give their readers an impression that Branwell's whole life was a trial and disgrace to his family; whereas we know that only during the last three years, when he was suffering abnormal strain of physical and mental anguish, did he become a source of acute anxiety and distress to his father and sisters. For at least twenty-seven years he was the object of pride and dear affection.

Ten

A T AGE TWENTY-SIX, Branwell, after a few botched careers, joined his sister Anne who was employed by the Robinson family at Thorp Green, an estate near York. This last place of employment for Branwell would become his "death warrant." Anne was already established as governess for the Robinson daughters, and now Branwell was hired as their son's tutor.

Mr. Robinson was an invalid, and soon Branwell was having a secret love affair with Lydia Robinson, his employer's wife. Whatever the full story, Mr. Robinson discovered the affair, and Branwell was immediately ordered back to Haworth and forbidden any contact with the Robinson family or (according to Branwell) he would risk being shot.

Branwell could not endure the heartache of losing Mrs. Robinson (whom Reverend Brontë referred to as a "diabolical seducer.") It nearly drove him insane, and he never recovered.

Anne chose to also leave her employment with the Robinson family after her brother's dismissal. Poor Anne, who was already unhappy with her job, had to endure the humiliation of her brother's disgrace, yet in all her later writings, she never revealed details of the scandal.

(Some speculate that the 1967 movie *The Graduate* was based on Branwell Brontë and Lydia Robinson.)

When Mr. Robinson died, Branwell hoped to marry Mrs. Robinson, the "love of his life," but she had other plans, leaving Branwell to drown himself in booze and laudanum (opium.)

Shortly after Branwell's death, Mrs. Robinson married a wealthy man and became the titled Lady Scott.

Perhaps Branwell drank like a fish because he didn't have the strength of mind to be responsible for his sisters and aging father as would have been expected of him. To be financially responsible, he'd have to first be successful.

How was that to happen? He'd been raised like a hero who could do no wrong—the apple of the Brontës' eyes—yet what substantial training for success did he have in little Haworth?

Instead he dabbled in various activities—he engaged in local boxing, joined the Freemasons, and did a stint as the secretary of the Haworth Temperance movement!

There's an old story that Branwell was sent to the Royal Academy of Arts in London to seek his fame and fortune, but instead of arriving, he went on a drunken bender and came home with a sad story that he'd been robbed, a tale that's been laid to rest by Dr. Juliet Barker (*The Brontës*, 2010) as untrue.

A talented boy like Branwell should have been educated beyond the local children's school and beyond home schooling, as his sisters had been. His brilliant mind had nowhere to go, and subsequently, his employment, for which he wasn't well suited, didn't work out.

Charlotte Brontë was doubtful when Branwell was hired by the Leeds and Manchester Railway. That sounds judgmental, but in reality Charlotte knew her brother's talents would be wasted on a job where his creative juices had no fertile ground in which to develop.

Charlotte was right.

Branwell often slipped away from his "clerk-in-charge" railway post at the Luddendenfoot Railway station in Calderdale, West Yorkshire. He often skipped work, while leaving a porter in charge, and foolishly ignoring his railway post.

When the railway did an audit and found missing funds, Branwell was held responsible and fired for negligence.

While in Calderdale, near Halifax, Branwell became good friends with a railway engineer named Francis Grundy. After Branwell's death, Grundy joined Branwell's other friends in defending their mutual friend against mean-spirited Brontë biographers. Francis H. Grundy (*Pictures of the Past: Memories of men I have Met and Places I have Seen, 1879*) wrote:

> Soon after I came to Halifax, I made the acquaintance of a genius of the highest order, Patrick

Branwell Brontë, who was at least as talented as any member of that wonderful family. Much my senior, Brontë took an unusual fancy to me, and I continued, perhaps, his most confidential friend through good and ill until his death.

Poor, brilliant, gay, moody, moping, wildly excitable, miserable Brontë! No history records your many struggles after the good—your wit, brilliance, attractiveness, eagerness for excitement,—all good qualities which made you such "good company," and dragged you down to an untimely grave. But you have had a most unnecessary scandal heaped upon you by the author of your sister's Biographer which that scandal does its best to spoil.

This generous gentleman in all his ideas, this madman in many of his acts died at age twenty-eight of grief for a woman. But at twenty-two, what a splendid specimen of brain power running wild he was! What glorious talent he still had to waste!

Francis Leyland recorded the memory of yet another friend of Branwell's from his railway days, poet, William Heaton:

"He was," says Heaton," blithe and gay, but at times appeared downcast and sad; yet, if the subject were some topic that he was acquainted with, or some author he loved, he would rise from his seat, and, in beautiful language, describe the author's character, with a zeal and fluency I had never heard equalled. His talents were of the very exalted kind. I have heard him quote pieces from the bard of Avon, from Shelley, Wordsworth, and Byron, as well as from Butler's "Hudibras," in such a manner as often made me wish I had been a scholar, as he was. At that time I was just beginning to write verses. It is true I had written many pieces, but they had never seen the light; and, on a certain occasion, I showed him one, which he pronounced very good. He lent me books which I had never seen before, and was ever ready to give me information. His temper was always mild towards me. I shall never forget his love for the sublime and beautiful work's of Nature, or how he would tell of the lovely flowers and rare plants he had observed by the mountain stream and woodland rill. All these had excellencies for him; and I have often heard him dilate on the sweet strains of the nightingale, and on the thoughts that bewitched him the first time he heard one."

Alice Law wrote:

While at Luddenden Foot [railway station] Branwell made many local excursions up that lovely valley. He had friends in the neighbourhood at Hebden Bridge, and we hear from Mr. Leyland that sometimes "clerical visitors" called at his wooden shanty to hear his brilliant conversation. They invited him to their houses also, and it was here that Branwell paid a visit to Manchester Cathedral. But these excursions drew him away from his proper duties; he did not attend closely to his work as he ought to have done; frequently he left it in charge of his deputy; and he was undoubtedly careless in his accounts. The Company invited him to appear before them and explain these irregularities. They decided to terminate his engagement with them, and so, after two years of employment, ended Branwell's career as a railway clerk.

It was an ignominious ending, and it plunged him into the greatest gloom. He felt keenly the disgrace attached to his dismissal, all the more because it was such a disappointment to his family.

Emily and Charlotte were given funds to attend school in Brussels. Why wasn't Branwell given these same opportunities? No one today would be expected to carry the financial responsibility of his family, especially without training in some vocation. He was a portrait painter for a while, but that didn't work out either. He seemed to be a genius on the verge of developing his true skills, yet no one knew exactly *how* to encourage his path. They just expected that he should magically become a success.

It didn't help that Branwell was living in a fantasy world, imagining an easy life if he were to marry the wealthy Mrs. Robinson.

If Branwell had married and had his own family, it would have doubled an already heavy burden. And Branwell, being the only son, had an unspoken responsibility for his family's security because if Reverend Brontë should die, the Brontë siblings would be homeless.

Branwell wrote to his friend Leyland, sharing his wishful dreams of an easy life with Mrs. Robinson—'I had reason to hope that ere very long I should be the husband of a Lady whom I loved best in the world, and with whom, in more than competence, I might live at leisure to try to make myself a name in the world of posterity, without being pestered by the small but countless botherments, which, like mosquitoes, sting us in the world of work-day toil.'

It's no wonder that Branwell pined over Mrs. Robinson. She not only held the key to Branwell's heart, she could have been the answer to his financial prayers.

Before *Wuthering Heights* was written, and after Branwell was dismissed from the Robinson household in 1845, he apparently told his friends he was writing a novel.

After Branwell's death, Francis Grundy wrote about Branwell and *Wuthering Heights*:

> . . . Indeed, it is impossible for me to read that story without meeting with many passages which I feel certain must have come from his pen. The weird fancies of diseased genius with which he used to entertain me in our long talks at Luddendenfoot, reappear in the pages of the novel, and I am inclined to believe that the very plot was his invention rather than his sister's.

From the chapter "Wuthering Heights—By Branwell?" in Alice Law's book, *Patrick Branwell Brontë*:

We must now examine the evidences of Branwell's actual known literary power and achievements, and the particular reasons for believing that he was the author of "Wuthering Heights."

It will be necessary to turn back again to the year 1845, and to the close of the month of July, when Branwell, summarily dismissed from his tutorship, had returned home, because it was during the months immediately following his return that his literary activities, already alluded to, have a special significance in connection with our enquiry.

During the time when so many of Branwell's critics suppose that he was giving his entire leisure to drink and dissipation, we have his own evidence, taken from a letter he wrote to his friend Leyland in September, 1845, less than two months after he left Thorp Green, that he has long been turning over a great literary project in his mind. This was the preparation of a novel in three volumes.

His words are as follows:

"I have, since I saw you at Halifax, devoted my hours of time, snatched from downright illness, to the composition of a three-volume novel, one volume of which is completed, and, along with the two forthcoming ones, has really been the result of half a dozen by-past years of thoughts about, and experience in, this crooked path of life. I feel that I must rouse myself to attempt something, while roasting daily and nightly over a slow fire, to while away my torments; and I know that, in the present state of the publishing and reading world, a novel is the most sale-able article. . . .

My novel is the result of years of thought; and if it gives the vivid picture of human feelings for good and evil, veiled by the cloak of deceit which must enwrap man and woman; if it records as faithfully as the pages that unveil man's heart in 'Hamlet' or 'Lear' the conflicting feelings and clashing pursuits in our uncertain path through life, I shall be as much gratified (and as much astonished) as I should be if, in betting that I could jump the Mersey, I jumped over the Irish Sea. It would not be more pleasant to light on Dublin instead of Birkenhead than to leap from the present bathos of fictitious literature to the firmly fixed rock honored by the foot of a Smollett or Fielding."

The letter went on, but the message was clear. Branwell did not *only* hit the pub after Mrs. Robinson, he attempted turning lemons into lemonade by writing a novel he'd spent much time contemplating. Could this be true? Could Branwell jump from the unknown to the likes of Smollett or Fielding, the successful writers of his period? *Could* he have become the J.K. Rowling of Victorian England? Perhaps at the end of the day, he did.

More food for thought from Alice Law:

The first reason for identifying the book with that novel on which no one disputes that Branwell was actually engaged, is very significant, though indirect. Just at the time when it ought to be have been completed, this strange, wild story, "Wuthering Heights"— a story answering so well to the tale Branwell was basing on the experience of human passions as tragic as those of "Lear" or "Hamlet"—suddenly appears from apparently nowhere, sheltered under the aegis of the literary pseudonym of "Ellis Bell." Surely this is more than a remarkable coincidence?

(Emily Brontë's pen name was Ellis Bell.)

Of Branwell's capacity to write "Wuthering Heights" none of his intimate friends, those at least who were acquainted with his marked abilities, had any doubt whatever.

More from Alice Law:

(Including quotes from *Wuthering Heights* by *Emily Brontë* (*Cassell 1890.*)

Let us now turn to the internal evidence of the book itself, and examine how far and in what respects it shows signs of distinctively masculine authorship, and of Branwell's authorship in particular. The very character of this terrible tale should convince any thoughtful or closely observant reader that no woman's hand ever penned "Wuthering Heights." Such, indeed, was the universal opinion of the press when it first appeared, and it may yet return to that opinion. The internal evidence is all against a woman's authorship, for over every page there hangs an unmistakable air of masculinity that cannot be evaded. If the story takes on a feminine aspect at times it is merely because the recital is for the time being put in the mouth of the old housekeeper, Mrs. Dean; and, in respect to the part dealing with the upbringing of the younger Catherine, I willingly concede that Emily Brontë may have helped considerably. But the whole conception of the story is, from start to finish, a man's, particularly so whenever Mr. Lockwood is represented as dealing directly with the story and nowhere is this more evident than in the first two or three chapters.

Before examining these pages I would draw the reader's attention to the description of Thrushcross Grange, as given by the young Heathcliff, who had, of course, never seen any place more civilized than the Heights Farm. "Ah! It was beautiful," he exclaims, "a splendid place carpeted with crimson, and crimson-covered chairs and tables, and a pure white ceiling bordered with gold, a shower of glass drops hanging in silver chains from the centre and shimmering with little soft tapers." Now, this description is so detailed that it must have been copied from a house visited by the writer. Branwell was well acquainted with the drawing room at Thorp Green, and it should also be noticed as a curious coincidence that the names of both these houses begin with the same two letters, so that either of them might be blanked as Th Gr.

Searching closely for minuter traces of masculine authorship, even in the first chapter, we come across tiny pieces of evidence pointing to the fact that the writer was not only a man but a scholar. Literally on the very threshold not merely of the story, but of the house itself, we meet with a Latin word which would scarcely be known to anyone not conversant with his Livy or his Virgil: I refer to the word "penetralium."

I do not think Emily Brontë knew much Latin, if any. Assuredly she was not an advanced student in the classics, as we know Branwell was. Only a classical scholar would have used the term to signify the interior of the house he was about to enter. Other Latin or classical allusions are: the "indigenae," referring to the surly natives of the country-side, and Catherine Earnshaw's remark that those who attempted to separate her from Heathcliff would "meet with the fate of Milo!" Of which "Milo" here is not clear, but the athlete of Crotona was probably in the author's mind. The allusion would be natural to a student of Ovid or Cicero, and familiar enough to Branwell, though not, I submit, to Emily Brontë, who was not "learned" so Charlotte tells us. We know from Mr. Grundy how fond Branwell was of introducing Greek, Latin or French words into his correspondence. Some other masculine expressions occur in the first chapters which no gentlewoman of the prim and prudish 'forties would have dreamt of using: the reference to the figures of Loves and Cupids over the doorways as "shameless little boys"; the account of the "ruffianly bitch" who tore Lockwood's "heels and coat-laps"; the term applied by Heathcliff to Isabella Linton—"pitiful, slavish, mean-minded brack"; the curious exclamation of Catherine Linton, "Oh! I'm tired—I'm stalled, Hareton!"

The curses, the brutal language, Heathcliff's outbursts about "painting the house-front with Hindley's blood!"; the reference to "a beast of a servant," Mrs. Dean's remark, "I could not half tell what an infernal house we had"; all these could never have been introduced into a first novel by a quiet reserved young woman like Emily Brontë. These coarse and wild expressions were written by a man who had heard many of them used, for they flow naturally from the mouths of his characters.

There are also some touches in the meditations of Mr. Lockwood which particularly suggest Branwell's personal experiences, and which would never occur to a woman-writer; the passage referring to Lockwood's little adventure at the "seaside" where he was "thrown into the company of a most fascinating creature," and, continues the description, "a real goddess in my eyes, as long as she took notice of me. I 'never told my love' vocally; still, if looks have language, the merest idiot might have guessed I was over head and ears, she understood me at last, and looked a return, the sweetest of all imaginable looks. And what did I do? I confess it with shame— shrunk icily into myself like a snail; at every glance retired colder and farther, till finally the poor innocent was led to doubt her own senses, and, overwhelmed with confusion at her supposed mistake, persuaded her mama to decamp. By this curious turn of disposition I have gained the reputation of deliberate heartless-ness; how undeserved, I alone can appreciate." Now, could this have been written by a woman: more than this, can anyone imagine it to have been written by Emily Brontë?

Other passages pointedly suggest Branwell's authorship; the description of the class of yeoman farmer, with many of whom he was undoubtedly acquainted, "with a stubborn countenance, and stalwart limbs set out to advantage in knee-britches and gaiters. Such an individual seated in his armchair, his mug of ale frothing on the round table before him, is to be seen in any circuit of five or six miles among these hills, if you go at the right time after dinner!"

Branwell knew the kind of men well, and had often visited them at the congenial hour, when he was strolling across the moors around Haworth. One feels this touch is direct from his hand.

I agreed with Alice Law's case for Branwell's authorship, yet objected to her opinion that a woman couldn't write such a shocking book as *Wuthering Heights*. Yet understandably her views reflect those severe Victorian times in which the Brontës lived, and the author herself was born a century before today's world.

However, her case examines not so much whether a man or a woman wrote *Wuthering Heights*, but whether the creator was Branwell or Emily.

The Brontë children had created imaginary worlds together from childhood. The two eldest, Charlotte and Branwell, had been close friends, co-authoring stories with intricate adventurous plots, "published" in hand-crafted miniature books and magazines.

Charlotte and Emily conceived plays at night when they should have been sleeping. Charlotte and Branwell created a world called Glasstown, which evolved into an imaginary kingdom, Angria. Emily and Anne participated in creations until they broke away from their elder siblings and created their own kingdom, Gondal. Charlotte, Emily, and Anne self-published a book of poems. Branwell was the first Brontë to be published in newspapers.

So is it really much of a stretch for Emily and Branwell to have collaborated on *Wuthering Heights*?

Eleven

My sister konni, who "spoke" psychically with John's spirit for many years before she passed away, had little insight into past lives beyond those of John and Katherine. The Brontës had been brought to my attention only occasionally, yet now I realize they were always lingering in the background.

Travelling to England on my first visit to Petworth, Sussex, in 1990, leaving my young family so I could search for my past life as Katherine, was a huge deal for me. I wrote in *All You Need Is Love* (2009):

I was days away from my departure. I was excited and nervous; everything was at stake. This would be the trip that would decide my fate, whether I would give up the whole search or carry it to the end.

My bags were packed, and everything was in order.

Minutes before leaving the house, Konni phoned. "Hi, I'm glad I caught you before you left. John just told me to remind you of the bluebells. He says you loved them. They grow wild . . . fields of them in the woods . . . maybe you'll see them."

"Bluebells," I laughed. "Okay, I'll add them to my list."

That trip in 1990 was like a dream. Years earlier I had written/channeled a story about Katherine's life. Initially, the story was never intended for publication, yet when visiting Petworth, I discovered that many names and places within the story had actually existed.

At the end of my week in Petworth, a helpful and friendly English woman (Ros Staker) took me on a little tour of the countryside, first showing me the remnants of an ancient bridge where possibly John and Katherine had crossed on their many Sunday afternoon excursions.

Ros pointed out a bluebell wood. I'd completely forgotten Konni's words about bluebells, and forgot about her words again until I learned that Emily Brontë and her sister Anne each wrote a poem of their love of the bluebell. (For me, this little connection seemed huge.)

I always seem to get ill right before Christmas. One year, when ill, my (now ex) husband brought home a heather plant, and it sparked a weird feeling within me. Despite wondering how he'd found a heather plant in our isolated mountain town in December, the plant seemed familiar.

When I was first divorced and worked at some difficult jobs in order to survive, I would imagine a purple/black sky and a wind howling over the earth. I loved my imaginary scene, and for several moments my workplace no longer existed.

Twenty years ago, in 1995, when I wrote *Just Imagine, a past life with John Lennon?* (the beginnings of *All You Need Is Love,*) I wanted to end the book with a poem by Emily Brontë, which I'd discovered in a book by Dr. Juliet Barker: *The Brontë Yearbook* (1990)—selected poems and writings by each member of the Brontë family.

I wrote to Dr. Barker, who kindly granted permission to use the poem. I was so happy to have Emily's poem as part of the book about John and Katherine, it just seemed natural.

In 2009, I truly began to "tune in" to John.

When Konni was alive, she would say, "He wants to speak with you himself," and I would always opt out by saying that she could receive his spirit communications better than I. But now I was on my own. Since arriving in Little England, I've received much guidance showing John's presence. In brilliant ways he shows himself: a little voice would say, *Pick up this book, go here, go there,* and it always ended up with Lennon, Baron, or Brontë information. I enjoyed the ride, but I was so caught up in the wonder of the signs that I often missed the actual messages.

When John said, *get re-acquainted with the Brontës*, I only half-listened. I didn't want to think about Emily, so I fooled myself into ignoring her and concentrating only on Branwell and John. In 2010, it had been sixteen years since first visiting the Brontës' home and the experience of knowing about the renovated kitchen.

In 2005 I met an English woman, Gerry, through an email. She contacted me after reading *All You Need Is Love*. Actually she was too shy to write herself, and the first contact came from her husband.

Over time, Gerry and I have become on-line pen-pals. She understands past lives, and after years of our corresponding, I mustered the nerve to ask if she had been Anne Brontë in her past life. (Charlotte's best friend, Ellen Nussey, said that Anne and Emily were "like twins.")

To me, Gerry felt like Anne, so it was a delightful surprise to learn that Anne Brontë's first surviving poem, included in Anne and Emily's fantasy world (Gondal) is titled "Verses by Lady Geralda."

Every year Gerry and her husband visit Haworth and Scarborough, where Anne Brontë is buried. It took Gerry a long time to share that indeed, she has felt (for years) that she's possibly reincarnated from the soul of Anne. And the more I know Gerry, the more clearly I see an obvious likeness between her and Anne.

Jewelle and Gerry outside the Black Bull Pub,
Haworth, Yorkshire, 2010.

Here is a passage taken from *In The Footsteps of the Brontës* (1914) by Mrs. Ellis H. Chadwick who describes Anne: "The old people of Haworth described her as gentle, sweet and good with very pretty features and long curls of light brown hair."

When Gerry and I met in Haworth, it *was* like we were sisters: it was lovely. We spent most of the day at the Parsonage, even gossiping about Charlotte and sympathizing

Anne Brontë—Portrait by Charlotte Brontë, 1834.
Credit: 'Courtesy of The Brontë Society.'

with Branwell. Then we laughed, listening to ourselves.

It was so special to be with Gerry in the Brontës' home. She had visited Haworth many times, sharing my own close feelings about the Brontës.

Inside the Parsonage I pointed to the Reverend Brontë's portrait. Did she think his eyes looked like John Lennon's?

"Yes," she laughed, "they *do!*"

Gerry accompanied me to the Black Bull Pub. Workmen were decorating Haworth for Christmas, and the village center resembled a scene from a Charles Dickens novel.

"Branwell's pub" was quiet and large.

Behind a massive bar, a man and woman were stringing Christmas lights. The low ceiling had huge, thick beams, and the view through the ancient pub windows revealed the charming village outside.

A Christmas tree stood beside a short flight of carpeted stairs that led to a roped-off landing displaying the famous chair once used by Branwell Brontë.

Gerry and I were in a cheerful mood, and it was exciting to see this piece of Brontë history.

I climbed the few stairs and was inches away from the

magnificent wooden chair with its circular arms. A sign said it had been Branwell's chair.

Seconds after gazing at the chair, a strong male spirit, seemingly in a flash, enveloped my body and mind. His manner was savage yet familiar, as if he could growl and get away with it. I was overwhelmed as his telepathic words saturated my whole being:

I was King in this chair. I was Somebody.

Stumbling back down the stairs into Gerry's arms, I sobbed uncontrollably.

In all the years of communicating with John, I'd never received a whisper from Branwell or even expected one. But now (perhaps), with his past-life sisters present in "his" pub, he had been waiting for this opportunity to justify to those who thought so highly of him, their brother, their hero, to answer their questions: Why did he destroy himself on those nights in the Black Bull Pub? Why did he break their hearts, forcing them to witness his fall from grace, their beloved brother whose life literally disappeared before them?

Emily, Anne, or Charlotte had never witnessed their

charming genius brother in the public houses: the story-teller, the witty life of the party, receiving admiration from his peers and mates. In this social environment he attained the recognition that the outer world expected of him, that his family desired for him. Here in the pubs of Haworth, he *was* the golden boy.

It's taken me four years to understand what happened that day when Branwell's brief, intense spirit-contact took place in the Yorkshire pub. In one thunderous moment, his past behavior was explained. No apologies, no regrets, just roughly spelled out as perhaps any brother could share with a close sister. Branwell still loved his sisters, and they deserved, on a soul level, his explanation. He *had* been King in that chair, in that pub, when he was the celebrity, when he was *a somebody.*

Perhaps like John/Branwell's need to explain his remorse to Jack, his past-life father, he also needed his sisters to understand their much-loved lost brother. In the years when Branwell was impossible to live with, each Brontë coped differently. Papa Brontë kept Branwell close at night, while probably praying, sharing a bedroom with his delirious and ranting son. Anne eased her mind by writing *The Tenant of Wildfell Hall* (*1848*), paralleling her observations of her brother's wayward lifestyle. Charlotte, in her displeasure and profound disappointment with her once-hero brother, before and after his death, could only express her deepest sorrow through letters.

(Source of letters: *The Brontës Life and Letters, Vol. 1, and Vol.2* Clement Shorter, Hodder and Stouughton,1908.)

On July 28, 1848, two months before Branwell died, Charlotte wrote to her dear friend, Ellen Nussey:

> Branwell is the same in conduct as ever. His constitution seems much shattered. Papa, and sometimes all of us, have sad nights with him: he sleeps most of the day, and consequently will lie awake at night.
>
> But has not every house its trial?

One week after Branwell's death, Charlotte, in a letter to her friend Mr. Williams, wrote:

My dear Sir,

We have buried our dead out of sight. A lull begins to succeed the gloomy tumult of last week. It is not permitted us to grieve for him who is gone as others grieve for those they lose. The removal of our only brother must necessarily be regarded by us rather in the light of a mercy than a chastisement. Branwell was his father's and his sister's pride and hope in boyhood, but since manhood the case has been otherwise. It has been our lot to see him take a wrong bent; to hope, expect, wait his return to the right path; to know the sickness of hope deferred, the dismay of prayer baffled; to experience despair at last—and not to behold the sudden early obscure close of what might have been a noble career.

I do not weep from a sense of bereavement—there is no prop withdrawn, no consolation torn away, no dear companion lost—but for the wreck of talent, the ruin of promise, the ultimate dreary extinction of what might have been a burning and shining light. My brother was a year my junior. I had aspirations and ambitions for him once, long ago—they have perished mournfully. Nothing remains of him but a memory of errors and sufferings. There is such a bitterness of pity for his life and death, such a yearning for the emptiness of his whole existence as I cannot describe. I trust time will allay these feelings. My poor father naturally thought more of his only son than of his daughters, and, much and long as he had suffered on his account, he cried out for his loss like David for that of Absalom—my son! my son!—and refused at first to be comforted.

And of Emily, biographer A. Mary F. Robinson wrote:

But there was one woman's heart strong enough in its compassion to bear the daily disgusts, weaknesses, sins of Branwell's life, and yet persist in aid and perfection. Night after night when Mr. Brontë was in bed, when Anne and Charlotte had gone upstairs to their room, Emily still sat up, waiting. She often had very long to wait in the silent house before the struggling tread, the muttered oath, the fumbling hand at the door, bade her rouse herself from her sad thoughts and rise to let in the prodigal, and lead him to safety to his rest. But she never wearied in her kindness. In the silent home, it was the silent Emily who had ever a cheering word for Branwell; it was Emily who still remembered that he was her brother, without that remembrance freezing her heart to numbness.

Five years before visiting Haworth and meeting Gerry, I obtained a psychic reading by Angela Challice. Throughout the reading, Angela was exceptionally "tuned in," so I couldn't resist asking her opinion of the idea that John Lennon was a later incarnation of Branwell Brontë.

"Hmm . . . Branwell," Angela mused. "He had sisters, didn't he? You *are* one of those sisters. You are Emily."

Angela seemed to forget about John and Branwell and began speaking of Emily, of how she could feel Emily's cold fingers as she wrote late into the night. Angela added,

"The Branwell Chair," Black Bull Pub, Haworth, Yorkshire.

"John is waiting for you to return to Haworth. He will meet you there. He's preparing for you to channel him."

I felt that was an outrageous statement—John's spirit meeting me in Haworth—but now I consider that if John and Branwell *are* the same soul, then indeed, he *was* waiting in Haworth at the Black Bull Pub to say his peace.

While in Haworth, I tried to keep Emily's spirit at bay, yet she slipped through anyway.

On a cold day with high winds and a spattering of rain, I struggled toward a path to the moors, stumbling like a cartoon character attempting to walk against the wind before finally accepting defeat. The day's storm continued into a black, wet night.

After dinner in the King's Arms Pub, I ran across the glistening cobblestoned lane beside the church for a final glimpse at the Brontës' home—the gray stone parsonage where Emily, Anne, Branwell, and Charlotte had written their works, creating their imaginary worlds, and where the Reverend Patrick Brontë grieved the deaths of each member of his young family.

I stood on the lane where Branwell had staggered drunkenly a hundred times, his genius soul trapped in a lifetime not yet ready for world recognition. The wind howled and rain blew in all directions as I stared up at the empty building. The night was *Wuthering Heights* weather indeed—raw, mystical, tormented. I loved it all.

Standing on the lane beside the Haworth church, gazing with longing at the empty Parsonage while the howling wind threw the cold, pelting rain in all directions, was my defining moment. Emily lives in some part of me. Or a part of me lives in her.

Twelve

*I*T WAS ONE THING to feel Emily within myself, but a year (or was it two years?) later, I felt I was living Emily's life. It was a bit disturbing, because I was losing the "me" that I knew, and someone else's life became my own. I began to love birds. Admire them. I was in awe of their beauty.

When I was a child, my father had bantam chickens. We kids loved eating their tiny eggs for breakfast. One day our pint-size rooster mistook my bare toes for his lunch, and I ran away screaming. From then on I was petrified of birds.

On learning of this fear, people would ask, "Have you seen the Alfred Hitchcock movie *The Birds*?" But it wasn't a movie that produced my phobia, it was the pecking rooster.

Then, as an adult, my fear turned to the ridiculous, and I avoided all birds. My youngest sister remembered shooing away pigeons for me at train stations in London when I was over thirty years old. It was embarrassing. So after being in Little England awhile, I had a sudden interest in the majestic eagles that soared over the nearby ocean and was in awe of the area's abundance of herons. I took pleasure in watching little birds in the garden.

One day I spoke to a little feathered fellow, and that's when it truly struck me. My life had become Emily Brontë's. In my heart of hearts, I knew that my sudden love of birds came from another time and place, for there was no way I would ever have loved birds. It was disturbing, because I didn't recognize myself anymore.

Of all the clues and evidence pointing to me as Emily, it was actually this sudden love of birds that convinced me. When the little birds splashed in Jack's garden birdbath or ate seeds from the bird feeder, I felt as if they were my friends. It was like looking at the world with someone else's eyes and feeling with someone else's heart. Then, like it or not, like John Lennon and Branwell Brontë's similarities, Jack and Papa Brontë's resemblances, and the connections between Anne Brontë and Gerry, I saw similarities between myself and Emily.

In 2009, before Gerry and I met in person, Gerry went on her yearly visit to Haworth with her husband. She picked a twig from a heather plant, the type Emily so loved, and posted it to me. When it arrived, I opened the package to discover purple heather in a plastic bag. With no time to think, I realized that my cheeks were covered in tears, as if someone had thrown a glass of water in my face. My body, in that gush of tears, had reacted violently to the twig of Yorkshire heather before my brain understood. Today, as I write, that sprig of heather lies beside my computer.

Emily, and her younger sister, Anne, were like best friends. Each year on Emily's birthday, July 30, she and Anne wrote private letters to each other, to be sealed and then read to each other four years later.

Throughout my life, in times of difficulty, I have written

letters to myself, sealing them, to be opened one year later. The idea was that when reading my words written twelve months earlier, it was a relief to know I'd survived!

Anne died in May 1849, five months after Emily's death. Years later, the sisters' last sealed birthday envelopes were discovered.

In 2009, Barry McGuinness, who was responsible for my examining a past life as Emily, sent me a portrait of Emily in her late twenties, near the time of her death. I'd never seen this portrait. The other portrait of her at age sixteen, painted by Branwell, had not resonated with me, although others saw a resemblance. The painter of this image later in Emily's life is unknown; Getty Images states that it dates from January 1847.

There is some controversy about this later image of Emily. Some say the portrait is not of her at all, but of an author, George Henry Lewes.

The strange thing (to me) is that the younger images

of George Henry Lewes look like my sister Konni when she was a girl, as if there's a family resemblance.

Despite the controversy surrounding this image of Emily, *I know that face.* Charlotte's reaction to George Henry Lewes (whom she didn't like) was surprising, as she too, "knew that face."

An oil painting of Emily Brontë (1818–1848), authoress of the novel 'Wuthering Heights,' published in 1847. (Photo by Hulton Archive / Getty Images) Credit: Hulton Archive / Stringer

In a letter (June 1850) to Ellen Nussey, Charlotte wrote:

I have seen Lewes. He is a man with both weaknesses and sins, but unless I err greatly, the foundation of his nature is not bad; and were he almost a fiend in character I could not feel otherwise to him than half-sadly, half-tenderly. A queer word the last, but I use it because the aspect of Lewes's face almost moves me to tears, it is so wonderfully like Emily—her eyes, her features, the very nose, the somewhat prominent mouth, the forehead—even, at moments, the expression. Whatever Lewes does or says, I believe I cannot hate him."

An English author introduced me to a psychic medium, and through a casual email correspondence, the psychic described her startling version of John Baron's seventeenth-century personality.

I was doubtful because I had no memories of John

being an aggressive, difficult man, yet the psychic said that only Kathy seemed to get along with him. It seemed strange that she called Katherine "Kathy," and her rough description of John seemed foreign to me.

Her description was reminiscent of an earlier (1990) psychic reading in Petworth. This psychic said the people of Petworth thought John was mad, and that he was not liked by the villagers. Apparently he had "ideas" about life that didn't sit well with the Sussex locals, as they simply couldn't relate to him.

Twenty years later, I learned that the Barons, a family of gentry, were also known as a political family. Perhaps this explained some of John's "mad ideas."

The new psychic summed up her analysis by describing John as a "Heathcliff" character. *Heathcliff?* This was shocking, and I blurted out that John Baron and John Lennon were possibly the same soul as Branwell Brontë. She replied that Emily Brontë and Katherine were of the same soul, and when Emily created the character of Heathcliff, she was subconsciously drawing on what others had thought of John Baron.

I didn't take this news to heart, because to me, John was never a Heathcliff, but coincidentally, that psychic's words were delivered on September 24, Branwell's death day. Was this a subtle sign?

I had to concur that possibly my love for John Baron, from Katherine's view, suppressed knowledge of his being a Heathcliff type, yet it did explain the earlier psychic's reading (from Petworth in 1990) that John Baron had rubbed some Petworth folk the wrong way, and that he wasn't liked by the locals.

For two years I researched Emily and Branwell and learned that there is little known about Emily, despite much speculation. We do know that Emily, like Branwell, lived in a mental fantasy land. Occasionally she left home to attend, or teach, at boarding schools, but acute homesickness always brought her back to Haworth. She couldn't survive away from home for long.

Emily had no social skills, yet Haworth villagers seemed

to have liked her, unlike students at various schools. Emily was tall (for a Victorian woman) and strong. Her huge mastiff, Keeper, on many occasions suffered severe discipline from her hand, followed by gentle compassion.

Once Emily broke up a dog fight in the village, and another time she beat poor Keeper with her bare hands after he was found sleeping on a white bedspread in an upstairs bedroom. No surprise that Emily's nickname was "the Major."

Keeper attended Emily's funeral, and it's said he howled beside her bedroom door for weeks after her death.

In the end, when all the Brontë children had died, Keeper was a beloved companion for the elderly Reverend Brontë.

The idea that I had been Emily in another lifetime seems preposterous to me on a bad day, yet possible on a more open-minded day. My problem accepting Emily as a possible past life was my inability to *feel* that she had written *Wuthering Heights*.

Without her novel, you are left with a girl who lost her mother and two elder sisters before the age of six, a distant father, a duty-bound and strict aunt, and siblings as friends and writing partners; a girl who wrote poems (self-published) and one book; a girl who couldn't survive in the outside world away from her beloved heather-covered moors; a girl who never knew romantic love, who loved birds, animals, the moors, heather, wind, and every aspect of the raw, natural world; a girl who was devoted to her brother and whose best friends were her sisters.

As with all the Brontë children, creating imaginary worlds through plays and stories, it was Emily who was said to have remained emotionally a child her whole life, dwelling in her fantasy world (Gondal) into her adult years. That much I could accept.

I believe Branwell Brontë was the genius behind *Wuthering Heights*. Is this why John led me to the Brontës—to set the record straight?

In an essay, "Spirit of the Moors," author Halliwell Sutcliffe wrote:

Had there been no Branwell Brontë to give a human meaning to the wild traditions, the wilder stories on which his sister fed, there had been no *Wuthering Heights*. Branwell is dead and the time to judge his faults are past—unhappy, sinning, seeking he knew not what tangled and miry paths, his memory has still some magic, some truth of spoiled romance. Nor was his life in vain—for out of his very sins and follies his sister made more threads than one from which to weave the finished piece called *Wuthering Heights*.

I asked for Jack's opinion of who he would trust with matters concerning Branwell—Branwell's loyal friends, or biographers like Mrs. Elizabeth Gaskell, who had never met the Brontë boy?

Jack said he would believe one's friends *always,* and to trust those who were actually *there*, who could paint a true picture. Wouldn't we all entrust our friends with our reputations and to be judge of our characters rather than a stranger, with agenda and loyalties directed elsewhere?

So when Spirit-John, who seems to be the same soul as Branwell Brontë, guided me toward the Brontë family, and when the reincarnation of other Brontë family members began to surround me, I knew this wasn't a lone journey. Therefore, to disregard Emily was foolish.

Somehow I feel and accept that my true love, John Baron, returned to me two hundred years later as my reincarnated brother.

It is said, "Behind every successful man is a woman." I believe that behind Emily's successful *Wuthering Heights* was Branwell. More so, I believe that Branwell and Emily wrote *Wuthering Heights* together.

Emily and Branwell, born eleven months apart, both musically inclined, were in tune with each other to the point of each writing a poem on the same day, on a similar subject, although Branwell was far from Haworth that day.

I believe Branwell created the genius outline for *Wuthering Heights*, and when he finally succumbed to sorrows, booze, and drugs, no longer caring for his/their saga, Emily knew how to complete the book.

Perhaps that psychic of years ago *was* correct when she said that Branwell and Emily's manuscripts are buried together. (The original manuscript of *Wuthering Heights* has never been located.)

Neither sibling knew that the saga of Heathcliff and Catherine would become a literary success, for this didn't happen until after brother and sister had died.

After Fiona, book designer/typesetter of the second edition of *All You Need Is Love*, offered me a job caring for her parents, I came to feel that one of those parents was my own past-life parent. And through *All You Need Is Love* I met my dear past-life sister (Gerry), who I believe is Anne Brontë.

Ultimately, the connections between John Baron/John Lennon/Branwell Brontë, Jack Brodie/Reverend Patrick Brontë, and Anne Brontë/Gerry finally left me no choice but to accept the possibility that I am Emily.

Ann Dinsdale, author of *The Brontës at Haworth* (2006), wrote: "When the novel, *Wuthering Heights,* failed to find a publisher, she was prepared to pay to see it in print."

In earlier years, Charlotte went snooping and, upon "discovering" Emily's poetry, decided the prose was good enough for publication. Emily was furious at the intrusion into her private world, but finally relented, at which time Anne, too, revealed her own poetry to her sisters. In order to remain anonymous, the girls agreed to choose male pseudonyms reflected in their initials. Charlotte became Currer Bell, Emily was Ellis Bell, and Anne was Acton Bell.

Only two copies of their poetry book sold. Self-publishing isn't an easy decision today, let alone in Victorian England. Their pen names were used in later novels, and Emily's real name wasn't attached to *Wuthering Heights* until after her death.

An American publisher announced that *Wuthering*

Heights and Anne Brontë's *The Tenant of Wildfell Hall* was written by Currer Bell. Obviously the male pseudonyms were causing confusion, so Charlotte and Anne went to London to enlighten their surprised publisher as to their real identities.

Ellis/Emily refused to accompany her sisters. Did she refuse because she was antisocial or because she knew she wasn't the true author?

In Emily's remaining years, while the others were busy making their own life plans, someone needed to stay home and care for Reverend Brontë. Emily was the obvious choice and became her father's housekeeper and nurse. In her spare time she wrote. *This exactly describes my current life.*

After Jack's wife passed, my life slowly become an isolated place where for days, weeks, and then months, there was no one to speak with except Jack, or perhaps a store clerk. My once busy world had morphed into a quasi-nineteenth-century housekeeper/nursemaid's life. I wrote when I could. My outer life was tedious but comfortable enough, yet my inner life was rich with spirit communication.

A psychic in Sussex once said, "You are like the ocean—a (non-eventful) life on the surface, with a tremendously rich inner life."

I seemed to have one foot in Emily's life. I wondered why I had been led there. How would I get my own life back? Branwell/John needed to make his peace with Jack, but surely there must have been another reason for my returning to the past, and slowly I began accepting that it *was* possibly my past too. I've learned so much from Jack, as I'd learned from his spiritual wife, Renee.

Shortly after my arrival in little England, I'd been working with a man who was developing a website, yet his costs increased nearly every day. Jack advised getting rid of him. "I'm not very good at confrontation," I said.

"Well, by the time you leave here, you *will* be," he replied. It seemed an odd remark at the time, yet it's proven to be true. I've learned a lot about the world from Jack.

Then there is Jack's daughter, Fiona. We truly connect on one topic: books. Once I mentioned to her about the little handmade books that the Brontë children created, with writing so tiny that only a child could read the text.

"Oh, I've made miniature books," Fiona said.

"You have?" I gulped.

The next week, she came to visit and handed me a bag containing two beautiful miniature books. She had made them herself—they were as beautiful as any professionally bound book. For a few seconds, my surroundings seemed surreal. I'd never heard of anyone who created handmade books except the Brontë children, John Lennon, and now Fiona.

Thirteen

Throughout my research, I had overlooked the childhood writings of the Brontës until I stumbled upon Branwell's fictitious characters in his and Charlotte's imaginary world, Angria. In this world of their own making, events seemed to show that Branwell, on a subconscious level, possibly remembered his past life as John Baron.

Branwell had named two of his fictional characters with actual names from John and Katherine's seventeenth-century world in Petworth: John Baron Flower and Alexander Percy, Earl of Northangerland.

Branwell had many pen names, his favourite being Northangerland. Others were John Bud, Captain John

Flower, Captain John Flower, M.P., and finally the Right Honorable John Baron Flower. Branwell also wrote under his own name, P.B. Brontë.

In 1834, at age seventeen, Branwell wrote *The Wool is Rising: An Angarian Adventure* by the Right Honourable John Baron Flower. The story's character is again Percy, Earl of Northangerland.

As I read the list of Branwell's stories, including those by the fictional Right Honorable Alexander Percy, Earl of Northangerland by John Bud, something seemed familiar.

The surname Percy is legend in Petworth, having been the surname of successive earls and dukes of Northumberland through the centuries.

The (real) Percy family home is Alnwick Castle. Branwell's favorite character, Alexander Percy, Earl of Northangerland, was his alter ego, and often Branwell named Alnwick as Percy's home.

Was it from past-life memory that Branwell gave his characters the names Percy and Northangerland—the same names from this most noble family in Petworth (and in all of England) and also using the name Northangerland

(a play on the name Northumberland) in different correspondence? Surely this was beyond coincidence! (Emily
too was known to use the name Percy in some poems.)

Up to his final days, Branwell used the nickname
Northangerland when writing notes to his friends, and
he even used the name when writing to newspapers.

Were John Baron's seventeenth-century memories so
significant (to him) that he carried his memories forward
two hundred years, to Branwell's nineteenth-century life?

The Percys were an ancient and wealthy family, first
arriving in England from France in the eleventh century.
Alnwick Castle in Northumberland has been the Percy
home for over seven hundred years. Petworth House, the
Percy's southern home for hundreds of years, was in Petworth, West Sussex, in Katherine James' home town.

Through twenty years of research about Petworth, I've
often noticed (while not giving it any relevance) the mention of a Lady Elizabeth Percy, who was one year older than
Katherine. Lady Elizabeth Percy, the only surviving child
of the 11th Earl of Northumberland, was born in January
1667, at Petworth House. She married very young, was

widowed twice, and by age sixteen was about to marry for the third time. Her third (Petworth House–related) marriage took place in May 1682, in the same month that John and Katherine fell in love at a ball in Petworth.

My book *All You Need Is Love* contains a channeled story, "Katherine's Story," written before I visited Petworth and learned that the names of people and places I had "made up" actually existed. My favorite memory was that of Katherine and John falling in love at a ball. From "Katherine's Story":

> I could see the ballroom as clearly as if I were dancing there right now. The hall was decorated with flowers, the air was warm, everyone was happy, or did they seem to be reflecting my happiness? If I could choose a frozen space in time to live, this is where I'd dwell forever. The hall was becoming hot from the dancing and the excitement in the air. John whispered, "Pray let us escape." Katherine followed him through the flowered archway outside, where the cool air caressed their faces. They fell

silent as they strolled along the stone terrace. The sky was clear. Bright stars shared the night with them. The moon was at its fullest, so lanterns were not needed.

Through my later research, I learned that in those days, events were planned around the full moon so that lanterns would not be needed for travelling by coach to social events. Also, the ball seemed quite extravagant for a village May Day dance. Might it also have been a ball to celebrate the marriage of Lady Elizabeth Percy? I have no evidence of that, except even today the nobility who live in Petworth House often invite the villagers of Petworth to celebrations.

The full moon in May 1682 occurred in the week of May 20, the probable time for the May Ball when "lanterns weren't needed" and when John and Katherine fell in love. Ten days later, on May 30, 1682, the Lady Elizabeth Percy married Sir Charles Seymour (who became the 11th Earl of Northumberland). The marriage took place in London and thereafter they settled in Petworth House.

After his marriage to Elizabeth Percy, the new earl built a new, grand Petworth House. Katherine and John both died before it was built. Were the May Ball— possibly in the old Petworth House, when John and Katherine fell in love—and the celebration of the wedding of nobility connected in John/Branwell's mind?

Either way, these events, the Percy wedding and my memories of the May Ball, according to the dates of the full moon, were approximately ten days apart. Lady Elizabeth Percy's new husband became the 11th Earl of Northumberland. John or Katherine had probably seen Lady Elizabeth Percy and Sir Charles Seymour in person and in their minds, connected the Percy marriage to their own romance.

Branwell remembered and created his imaginary character, Percy, the Earl of Northangerland, knowing full well this came from the name Northumberland. Meanwhile, did Emily and Branwell both subconsciously remember Katherine, as the psychic had said—"Catherine" who loves Heathcliff, a.k.a. John Baron? And did John Lennon remember Branwell Brontë's life, explaining why a song by Yoko Ono, released after John's death, contains the mention of Heathcliff and Catherine?

My theory is that Branwell, who lived two hundred years after John Baron lived, subconsciously remembered and created his alter-ego from real people from seventeenth-century Petworth. This helps answer some questions that otherwise would have to be explained as coincidence:

Was Branwell remembering those *very names* from his past life as John Baron? Did he change his pen name from John Flower to John *Baron* Flower because he remembered his lifetime as John Baron? Did Branwell mean John Baron as a surname or Baron as a title? Either way it seems beyond coincidence.

If the psychic was correct, and John *was* a Heathcliff-type character, and if John and Katherine, as Branwell and Emily, were remembering their past lives when together they created *Wuthering Heights*, then this accounts for my being sent to Jack's home. The only place these memories (for Emily) could flourish was in a "Brontë home." If Jack, now reincarnated, was Branwell's father from the past, then he was also Emily's past-life father.

There's no way in this lifetime I would have seriously accepted that I had once been Emily Brontë if I'd not returned, literally, to live in the home of the once head of the "Brontë family." I wasn't sent to Jack's home solely because of Branwell and John, I was sent here to remember who I am: not a famous author, for that happened after Emily's death, but to remember who both John and I were, a discovery that began with the Petworth past life. That lifetime was one side of the coin, the Brontë lifetime, the other. Or so it seems.

The pain of loss wasn't healed in John and Katherine's lifetime together, nor in Emily and Branwell's lifetime, so the unlikely occurrence of being sent to Little England (I believe) was to finally put to rest the two losses in Katherine's and Emily's lives.

This life of mine, since age twenty-seven, has been unusual. Although I don't completely understand *why*, I know there's a larger reason playing itself out for my spiritual development. We each must travel the individual road of our soul's journey.

Through the years I've had several past-life regressions.

All journeys to the past are different in their unfolding, and I do *not* enjoy the experience. Scenes appear in fits and starts and are always a surprise. Undergoing past-life regressions is hard work.

In 2012, psychic and friend Glenna Quinn gifted me with a past-life regression for my birthday. Earlier, I'd made a decision never to undergo any more such regressions, but because of her generosity, I accepted.

In past-life regressions, a facilitator puts you into an altered, relaxed state, and often begins with a suggestion to (mentally) enter a hallway and chose a door (a lifetime) to open.

Years ago in a regression I saw the number 1848 emblazoned on one door, yet I chose not to enter. That was the death year of both Emily and Branwell, and I didn't want to "visit" that time period. Later I envisioned a return to the Brontës' life, if that was possible. What would I see? Emily writing *Wuthering Heights?* Emily walking on the moors with her huge mastiff in tow? Or Charlotte and Anne, would they be there? Or would I see a little girl who grieved for her deceased mother and two beloved sisters? Or an older Emily with an intelligent yet distant father, or an over-emotional, talented brother?

Glenna orchestrated a gentle yet powerful session. I felt completely relaxed as she "took" me to a hallway with doors of many colors. This time no doors were adorned with the number 1848, thus enhancing my relaxation. I chose a thick wooden door with a brass knocker—it seemed the same heavy door that had once evoked memories when I visited (for real) an ancient hospital in Sussex back in the nineties.

Oh, we're going to Petworth. The thought filtered through my altered state as I lay under a fuzzy blanket on a Reiki table in Glenna's beautiful sanctuary room.

I mentally pushed open the solid wood door. I had entered an old church, but instead of viewing old Petworth, I was attending Branwell's funeral! My body felt as if it was convulsing, and sobs wracked within my chest. I was shaking and my temperature seemed to drop. Then I understood. I have grieved in three known lifetimes over John's death—Baron, Brontë, and Lennon.

Katherine died months after John. Emily died of consumption three months after Branwell's death. And after Lennon was shot to death, my own life, turned upside down, no longer existed.

Fourteen

*B*RANWELL DIED on September 24, 1848. Six days later his obituary appeared in an eight-page Yorkshire newspaper, now archived at *The British Newspaper Archive*. Other obituaries in the same small newspaper were written in a matter-of-fact style, yet reading Branwell's shows that he was obviously much loved by many.

Reading the newspaper on-line is painstakingly slow, forcing one to read line by line and page by page. This turned out to be a blessing; otherwise I would have missed a heart-stopping "coincidence."

On the front page of the Saturday 30 September 1848 edition of *The Leeds Times* was an ad for a new clothier business opening in Leeds by a tailor/clothier/general outfitter/woollen draper named John Barran.

The name coincidence was startling, especially since "my" John Baron's seventeenth-century family were wool merchants.

On the second page of the newspaper was an ad for a newly released book by London author R.J. Brodie (Jack's name—J. Brodie!).

All three of these significant (to me) names—John Barran's clothier ad, R.J. Brodie's book, and Branwell Brontë's obituary on page eight—have sat quietly for over one hundred and sixty years in a small Yorkshire newspaper.

If I had any doubts about these past and present connections, this centuries-old newspaper spoke to me. And perhaps reading between the lines of this heartfelt tribute amongst the obituaries tells us more about Patrick Branwell Brontë than what a hundred biographies could.

On Sunday morning last, at the Parsonage, Mr. Bramwell Brontë (sic), son of the Rev. P. Brontë incumbent of Haworth. This announcement will, no doubt, be read with sincere regret, by those in different parts of the country who had the pleasure of his acquaintance, he having been extensively known from the situation he formerly held on the Leeds and Manchester Railway, and since then, as a tutor in a gentleman's family, near York; he has however, lately lived with his father and sisters at the Parsonage, Haworth. The talents and accomplishments of this young gentleman have very rarely been excelled. Gifted with great natural quickness, an acute perception, and a solid judgment, he was, so far as his mental endowments were concerned, admired by all who knew him, while his bland and urbane manners, and remarkable conversational powers, charmed and captivated all by whom he was surrounded. His premature death—in his 31st year—has thrown his aged and respected father, and three sisters, into the deepest sorrow, and his friends are ready to acknowledge that the brightest ornament of their social circle is gone. His mortal remains were conveyed to their final resting place, in Haworth church, on Thursday last, amidst a crowd of sympathising spectators.

Months ago an email arrived from Amazon.com with an ad for a book: *What Type am I? Discover Who You Really Are.* The author's name was Renee Baron.

I'd forgotten about finding the book in the thrift shop that day: *Do What You Are*—one of the authors' was named Barbara Barron.

In the same week as the "Baron email," on a soul-searching day, I wandered through town with no destination, asking myself, "Could I *really* write a book and speak about Emily Jane Brontë?"

Absentmindedly, I entered a drug store and on the wall were gigantic words: *Be Yourself.* And if that wasn't the last straw, a friend brought me a gift later that week: a pen with the inscription *Emily.*

Now I understood the flashing neon message in New York. *A Leap of Faith.* My spiritual development required that I take a gigantic leap of faith to the next level, because *really,* writing about Emily Brontë and myself was the last thing on earth I would, or *could*, ever do. And here I am, choosing to do so. But who am I kidding? Spirit-John has cajoled me into "owning" my past life, a lifetime when he and I lived in that creative family in northern England, isolated from the world, nearly two hundred years ago.

As my granddaughter posed on our final day in New York, "It's like you and John have one chance to do something together in this lifetime."

John Lennon and the Brontë Connection is the direction that *All You Need Is Love* was always heading toward.

John Lennon was violently murdered when I was twenty-seven. I am now sixty-two. It's taken my whole adult life to know myself.

In response to author Alice Law's question from more than one hundred years ago, "What became of Branwell's undoubted genius?"

Patrick Branwell Brontë's soul lives on, once reborn as a wee boy in Liverpool, England, a boy who felt unloved, yet taught the world that love is all there is. John Baron, Branwell Brontë, and John Lennon are three men of one soul.

Or so I believe.

circa 1840: Poet and artist Branwell Brontë (1817–1848),
brother of the Brontë sisters. Silhouette from the Brontë Museum.
(Photo by Hulton Archive / Getty Images)
Credit: Hulton Archive / Stringer

Afterword

By France Allion
Near Phoenix, Arizona

*I*N THIS WORLD there are many who walk their paths without too much thought. From time to time, an event catches them by surprise and for an instant, they are made to realize their uniqueness, because, as we know, it's through travail that insight occurs. It is at this time that we may rise up to meet our potential.

This author, Jewelle St. James, on the other hand, has struggled for over two decades to acquaint herself with her own uniqueness. As her research revealed what she was unable to completely embrace, Jewelle kept insisting on anonymity. Against accumulating evidence, year after

year, I, along with friends and family, watched her continue to try to back away from the obvious: her history
with that person known in this lifetime as John Lennon.

Despite her internal conflict, Jewelle's travels went
on relentlessly to those parts of the British Isles that gave
up their history, their secrets, that chunk by chunk built
the evidence of linkage between her and he who was first
known in seventeenth-century England as John Baron.

With great determination and spirit, confronting the
emerging scraps of evidence with deep skepticism, Jewelle walked her path of doubt. And as the Universe is wont
to provide, she finally was able to accept the veracity, the
undeniable truth of her several lifetimes with an historical figure who, in his nineteenth-century incarnation,
struggled with his own identity, his abilities, his destiny:
Branwell Brontë, progenitor of John Lennon.

It is in this figure, Branwell Brontë, that the puzzle
begins to finally pull itself together. As is commonly the
occurrence, we each of us, time after time, return as part
of a Soul family. Tracing the John Lennon lineage backward, we find him in the figure first as John Baron. Later,

in the 1800s, he surfaces as Branwell Brontë and we learn of him as both a gifted individual and a conflicted, seemingly undirected individual. The son of a stern and disciplined father/minister, Branwell was admired locally by all who knew him. As the brother of three author-sisters, despite his undisciplined ways, he too was thought to be author and producer of some printed materials.

It is at this point that again the monster of doubt raises its bewildering head to Jewelle. Despite the obvious connection between her historical characters and John, nevertheless her mind could not, would not succumb to the developing fact that she was one of Branwell's sisters, Emily. However, now we can see her "evolution" from Katherine of the seventeenth-century to Emily of the nineteenth-century.

Now we can, with certainty, recognize not only the Lennon-Brontë connection, but the Katherine-Emily connection. Of course! History is not a willing deceiver; in reincarnation the connections are reliable. When we are given, after years of work and effort, the final answer, how can we not readily grasp it?

It is to Jewelle's ongoing credit that today we see the results of her quest. Despite her own overwhelming doubts, she has finally given us the picture of what had been staring us in the face: she as Emily and John as Branwell, once again sharing a lifetime together.

The beauty of these many facts of the story unfolds completely in this edition. We can experience the love that has accompanied these two figures throughout their lifetimes. Is it any wonder that this author was so life-changingly affected by the death of John Lennon? So affected by the death of a family Soul member that her whole life turned upside down and did a complete about-face? So affected that her life mission became one of "unravelling" this universal mystery?

What an accomplishment! What a feat of sheer determination and will power! What a miracle of life and a revelation of the workings of the Universe!

Now we can clearly see these workings and discern their importance. Jewelle has uncovered not only her soul's history, but in fact, the path that we all walk, the journey that we are all on: knowing our many selves down through the centuries.

It is only through this door that we come to know self-acceptance and peace. It is only through accessing this door that we succeed in knowing ourselves, freeing ourselves, and thereby freeing up our regard for others.

By coming to and through the door of self-forgiveness and reaching that door of complete comprehension with the name *PEACE* on it do we approximate the peace that John Lennon sang of, dreamed of, and worked toward; the peace that can someday come to the world as each of us finds it within our own consciousness. Without self-peace there can be no world peace. Let us all work toward that incredible and sacred goal.

Bibliography and Further Reading

Barker, Juliet. *The Brontës*. Abacus, 2010.

Barker, Juliet. *The Brontës: Wild Genius on the Moors: The Story of a Literary Family*. New York: Pegasus Books, 2012.

Barker, Juliet. *The Brontë Yearbook*. London: George Weidenfeld & Nicolson Limited, 1990.

Baron, Renee. *What Type am I? Discover Who You Really Are*. Penguin Books, 1998.

Brontë, Anne. *The Tenant of Wildfell Hall*. Penguin Classics, 2012.

Brontë, Charlotte. *Jane Eyre*. New York: HarperCollins. 2010.

Brontë, Emily. *Wuthering Heights*. London: Penguin,1995.

Chadwick, Mrs. Ellis H. *In the Footsteps of the Brontës*. London: Pitman, 1914.

Chitham, Edward. *A Life of Emily Brontë*. (Amberly Publishing, 2012), Kindle Edition.

Dinsdale, Ann; Simon Warner. *The Brontës at Haworth.* London: Francis Lincoln, 2006.

Du Maurier, Daphne. *The Infernal World of Branwell Brontë.* New York: Doubleday and Company Inc., 1961.

Frank, Katherine. *A Chainless Soul: A Life of Emily Brontë.* Boston: Houghton Mifflin, 1990.

Gaskell, Elizabeth. *The Life of Charlotte Brontë.* Edited by Elisabeth Jay. London: Penguin, 1997.

Gerin, Winifred. *Anne Brontë.* London: Nelson, 1959.

Gerin, Winifred. *Branwell Brontë.* London: Nelson, 1961.

Gerin, Winifred. *Emily Brontë.* Oxford University Press, 1971.

Grundy, Francis H. *Pictures of the Past: Memories of Men I have Met and Places I have Seen.* London: Griffith and Farran, 1879.

Hall, Judy. *The Hades Moon.* York Beach, ME: Samuel Weiser, Inc., 1998.

'Imelda's mission to revive Brontë Story.' Huddersfield Examiner. http://www.examiner.co.uk/news/west-yorkshire-news/imeldas-mission-revive-bronte-story-5064420 (accessed March 29, 2015).

"John Lennon." New World Encyclopedia, http://www.

newworldencyclopedia.org/p/index.php?title=John_ Lennon&oldid=979857 (accessed March 29, 2015).

Law, Alice. *Patrick Branwell Brontë.* London: A.M. Philpot, 1923.

Lennon, John; Hunter Davies. *The John Lennon Letters.* Little, Brown and Company. New York, 2012.

Lewisohn, Mark. *Tune In: The Beatles: All These Years, Volume 1.* New York: Crown Archetype, 2013.

Leyland, Francis A. *The Brontë Family, With Special Reference to Patrick Branwell Brontë, Volume One and Two.* London: Hurst and Blackett, 1886.

"Soul mates: The reincarnation of Emily Brontë?" McGuinness., Barry. 2011, http://personalityspir ituality.net/2011/12/18/soul-mates-the-reincarna tion-of-emily-bronte/ (accessed March 29, 2015).

Riley, Tim. *Lennon: The Man, the Myth, the Music—The Definitive Life.* New York: Hyperion, 2011.

Robinson, A. Mary F. *Emily Brontë,* 2nd ed. London: W.H. Allen and Co., 1883.

Ross, John J. *Shakespeare's Tremor and Orville's Cough—The Medical Lives of Great Writers.* New York: St. Martin's Press, 2012.

Shorter, Clement. *The Brontës: Life and Letters, Volume One and Two*. London: Hodder and Stoughton, 1908.

Shorter, Clement King. *Charlotte Brontë and her Circle*. London: Hodder and Stoughton, 1896.

Simpson, Charles. *Emily Brontë*. London: Country Life Ltd. New York: Charles Scribner's Sons, 1929.

St. James, Jewelle. *All You Need Is Love, Second Edition*. St. James Publishing, 2009.

St. James, Jewelle. *The Lennon-Brontë Connection*. St. James Publishing, 2011.

Sutcliffe, Halliwell. "Spirit of the Moors," in *Charlotte Brontë, 1816–1916; A Centenary Memorial (1917)*. Edited by Butler Wood. London: T.F. Unwin, 1918.

Tieger, Paul D.; Barbara Barron. *Do What You Are— Discover the Perfect Career for You Through the Secrets of Personality Type*. New York: Little, Brown and Company, 2007.

Wilson, Romer. *All Alone, The Life and Private History of Emily Jane Brontë*. London: Chatto & Windus, 1928.